Employment and Training R&D

R&D

Lessons Learned
and
Future Directions

Conference Proceedings
of
The National Council on Employment Policy

January 26-27, 1984

R. Thayne Robson
Editor

1984

The W. E. Upjohn Institute for Employment Research

Library of Congress Cataloging in Publication Data

Main entry under title:

Employment & training R & D.

   1. Manpower policy—Research—United States—Evaluation
—Congresses. 2. Occupational training—Research—United
States—Evaluation—Congresses. I. Robson, R. Thayne.
II. National Council on Employment Policy. III. Title:
Employment and training R and D.
HD5702.5.U5E56   1984   331.12'042'0973   84-7584
ISBN 0-88099-017-1
ISBN 0-88099-018-X (pbk.)

The National Council on Employment Policy is a private, nonprofit organization of academicians and policy experts with a special interest and expertise in the area of employment and training. This policy statement represents the combined judgment of the Council members. Despite a divergence of opinion on details, the members agreed to a unanimous statement.

Appraising Employment and Training Research

A Policy Statement
of the
National Council on Employment Policy
April 1984

The Manpower Development and Training Act of 1962 (MDTA) began a new era for labor market-related research by authorizing specific sums of federal money for research on the nation's employment and training problems. The Comprehensive Employment and Training Act continued that practice, and the Job Training Partnership Act of 1982 (JTPA) declares that the goal of the act is:

> Sec. 221. (a) To assist the Nation in expanding work opportunities and assuring access to those opportunities for all who desire it, the Secretary shall establish a comprehensive program of employment and training research utilizing the methods, techniques, and knowledge of the behavioral and social sciences and such other methods, techniques, and knowledge as will aid in the solution of the Nation's employment and training problems.

The use of the limited research and development (R&D) funds has been carefully planned and monitored, and the returns in policy improvement have been impressive. Nevertheless, this long-standing, high-payoff program, which is administered by the Department of Labor's Employment and Training Administration (ETA), appears about to be sacrificed on the altar of misplaced economy. Hence, it seems timely to review the nature and results of the program and identify those components especially worthy of saving.

Illustrative Contributions of ETA's
Research, Development, and Evaluation Program

ETA's research, demonstration, and evaluation (RD&E) program played an important role in changing the direction of the MDTA shortly after it was passed. The original legislation was enacted in response to the belief that automation was the major cause of unemployment during the 1960s. The Act directed the Department of Labor to provide training and retraining to persons with fairly strong attachments to the labor force whose skills had become obsolete as a result of technological changes.

Some of the earliest research supported under the MDTA suggested that automation was playing only a limited role in explaining the extent and nature of unemployment during the mid-1960s. The researchers clarified the problem of unemployment by directing the attention of policymakers to the growing number of disadvantaged workers who were jobless (i.e., minorities, women, youth, the uneducated and unskilled) and needed training and retraining to become employable. Those findings contributed to a redirection of policy, which has prevailed to this day. The finding that training applicants could not be successfully trained by existing methods because they could not read or write led to the addition of basic literacy courses to the program. When research showed that training programs were being inundated with inexperienced, jobless young school dropouts who were not eligible for training—the first wave of the baby boom—the rules were changed to enlarge the youth component. When other findings suggested that a high program dropout rate was related to inadequate stipends because many trainees could not afford to remain in programs, amendments were passed to augment those allowances.

Even as the emphasis changed to the disadvantaged, policymakers failed to realize that those services alone might not solve deep-rooted and pervasive problems, such as discrimination, the inability to read or write, inadequate labor market information, poor motivation, and insufficient market demand. The complexity of the social and economic problems faced by unemployed workers was brought to the attention of policymakers and the general public by the research, experimental and development program.

The findings of the RD&E program suggested that the assignment given to federal agencies to move unemployed workers into jobs was far more difficult to achieve than had been assumed in the early 1960s.

Social scientists supported under ETA's research program gave early warnings during the 1960s and the 1970s that profound changes were taking place in society that would affect women's participation in the labor force. They identified the growing divorce and separation rates, the increase in infants born to women without husbands, and the women's liberation movement as significant factors that would increase the number of women heading families who would be entering the labor force. Again, the research results were utilized for policy purposes, as reflected in new amendments to employment and training legislation and the design of new training programs for women who head families.

The labor market problems faced by minority workers were given special attention under ETA's social science research program. One significant study documented discriminatory practices that prevented minority enrollment in apprenticeship programs. The study also found that because minority youths have no relatives or other adult models in the skilled trades, they know very little about the apprenticeship system and how to enter it. In response, ETA funded an action-oriented organization to assist minority workers in learning about the apprenticeship system and prepare them for apprenticeship examinations. These efforts generated by the research are largely responsible for tripling the proportion of minority workers in apprenticeship programs between 1967 and 1980.

Long term support was provided to Columbia University's Conservation of Human Resources. The Columbia researchers were among the first to identify the role of government and other nonprofit institutions in economic growth. They also examined the impacts of the growing service-oriented sector and the effect of employers' policies on the employment experience of noncollege-trained young workers. A series of studies of the health industry correctly anticipated the rapid employment growth in the health field; these findings were used by program operators in selecting growth occupations for government-sponsored training of unemployed workers. Several examinations conducted by the Columbia group of the experience of other countries in dealing with training disadvantaged workers also helped to shape U.S. legislation and policies during the 1970s.

Early on, it became clear that progress in labor market research was being hampered by the lack of qualified researchers interested in the field. To develop research capabilities, ETA provided research support for over 500 doctoral candidates between 1962 and 1980 to induce young scholars to devote their talents to the study of employment and training problems. A conscious effort was made to bring new interdisciplinary skills into a field that had previously been limited largely to labor economists. The conclusions of many researchers funded by ETA indicated that employment and training problems transcended economics. Many of the scholars supported under this program are now employed in universities, private industry, foundations, government, and research organizations.

Mindful of the operational responsibilities, the managers of the RD&E program did not shrink from the independent evaluation of the agency's activities. They funded assessments of the Neighborhood Youth Corps (NYC), the Job Corps, and the Employment Service. An intragency committee consisting of departmental program officials and the research office developed research objectives for improving the services provided by the Labor Department. Research findings from these projects led to the creation of new NYC delivery models for rural youth and an employment service that was more responsive to the needs of the country's disadvantaged workers.

Research also saved money. The RD&E office helped design experimental and developmental models to pretest programs before they were introduced as large scale social programs. Coaching, outreach, and job development efforts had their origins in experimental and developmental projects. The experimental tests also prevented policymakers from embarking on impractical training approaches.

ETA research administrators were often able to persuade other federal agencies to underwrite experimental and demonstration projects. An example is the Supported Work project, which was cofunded by the National Institute on Drug Abuse, the Department of Justice, the Department of Health and Human Services and the Ford Foundation. This demonstration research project, which served 10,000 participants, was designed to develop a work alternative to welfare for persons often considered unemployable because of their antisocial behavioral patterns. Ex-offenders, ex-addicts, welfare heads of household, and unemployed, out-of-school youth were provided with work experiences for about a year, under close supervision and in a work situation associated with a crew of peers.

The Supported Work project indicated that diverse services were most effective in preparing women who had been long term welfare recipients for the world of work. The services also had an impact on a significant segment of the ex-addict population, but little effect on ex-offenders and the youth group. Although the major findings of the project have not been applied on a larger scale because of reduced federal funding for employment and training programs, several cities have adopted the model, and social service agencies have implemented projects for mentally retarded youth based on the findings of the Supported Work project.

In addition to mission- and problem-oriented research, the administrators of ETA's research program recognized that some social research requires a long term investment to illuminate complex economic and social developments. Therefore, in response to limitations of cross-sectional data that provide a snapshot of how workers fare in labor markets, ETA launched the National Longitudinal Survey (NLS) of labor market experience. Data were collected on the employment, unemployment, mobility, and other labor market experiences of a national sample of youth, middle-aged, and preretirement mature workers at various critical stages of their working lives. The NLS has provided insights into how, when, and why socioeconomic problems arise and has given scholars and policymakers important tools for determining future labor market decisions of workers. In 1979 a new cohort project was started which focused on disadvantaged youths and provided a follow-up of young persons who entered the armed forces.

The NLS is probably the most important data set that has ever been collected about American workers. The research findings have had important impacts on policy decisions and have affected the design of employment and training programs. For example, the NLS shows that lack of vocational guidance and vocational information handicaps young blacks in their job search efforts. NLS findings have repeatedly documented the effect of sex and race discrimination on women and minority workers. The data have shown that mature black women who are heads of one-parent families are among the most disadvantaged persons in our society. Hundreds of scholars have also used the unique information base of the NLS in studying the movement of workers into and out of the labor market.

The trend toward early retirement is confirmed by the NLS. The data indicate that, contrary to popular belief, the majority of men retire voluntarily, and only a small proportion are forced out of their jobs because of mandatory retirement; more than a third retire because of poor health. If funding continues, the NLS data will eventually be the nation's most significant source of information about mature working women as they approach retirement age.

Many of the NLS findings suggest that conventional employment and training approaches have not taken into account that many labor market disadvantages appear to originate in a long term developmental process that begins in the home. Values, attitudes toward work, family responsibilities, parental models, divorces and separations, sex role norms, age of marriage, and education and income of parents all seem to affect future labor market experiences. If the information from the NLS were applied, our human resource policies would call for training programs that place greater emphasis on preventing labor market disadvantages from developing at an early stage in an individual's life.

Managing the RD&E Program

In conducting a pioneering federal social science research program, the administrators of ETA had to design a procurement system that was equitable to those seeking research support, attract the most qualified personnel, and develop a staff capable of initiating, processing, and monitoring projects that could help ETA achieve its objectives. To complement those goals, the RD&E office encouraged the submission of unsolicited proposals, but it also initiated a competitive request for proposals (RFP). Originally, owing to funding limitations, greater reliance was placed on unsolicited proposals that came primarily from the academic community. When the RD&E budget was increased, experimental and demonstration projects were undertaken and more use was made of RFPs, which elicited proposals from entrepreneurial or consulting organizations.

An effort was made to maintain a balance between unsolicited proposals and RFPs in order to attract academically based scholars, who were more likely to question the premises on which programs and practices were based, and specialists employed in consulting firms who could apply their operational knowledge to experimental and development projects. Departmental staff, specialists employed in other federal agencies, and outside experts reviewed and assessed the proposals.

ETA offered academicians temporary fellowships to work in RD&E. These academicians became a valuable resource when they returned to their universities. Many of them contributed to policy-oriented research and assisted in formulating research issues and evaluating RD&E projects.

Dissemination and Utilization
of Research Findings

Censorship is a recurrent problem in federal agencies that sponsor social science research. Findings of research or experimental and development projects often question conventional wisdom or challenge the effectiveness of programs. Agency administrators often are not interested in publishing information that may be critical of programs they originated or manage.

Administrators of RD&E programs have had to protect the right of researchers to freely express conclusions based on their studies. They also play an important role in providing communication links between the research community and the potential users of research findings. ETA has published and disseminated research reports that were used in the policymaking process. A conscientious effort was made to translate the jargon of some social scientists so that research findings could be understood and used by a wide audience of policymakers and the general public.

Threats to Employment and Training Research

Over the past two decades, the National Council on Employment Policy has carefully assessed the RD&E programs that have been conducted by the Department of Labor's Employment and Training Administration. The Council has concluded that the products of ETA's social science research programs have played an important role in shaping and formulating national policy on employment and training issues.

We are therefore deeply concerned that the program is now facing the most devastating threats in its 20 years of productive existence. Funding has been cut from a modest 1980 level of $13.0 million to only $6.1 million for 1984. An excessive reliance on formal RFPs may encourage research that represents the preconceptions of politically appointed administrators, precluding innovative proposals based on the insights of objective observers. The doctoral dissertation program has been cancelled, cutting off the flow of new researchers. Policymakers and the general public of the mid- and late-1980s will not have access to the information needed to assess the effectiveness of the Job Training Partnership Act; such information can only be gleaned from the findings of academic-based researchers and the experts employed in consulting firms.

The recent discontinuance of the ETA Office of Research and Development's utilization and dissemination activities has created a serious vacuum in the knowledge base about the new direction of policy on employment and training issues.

The situation is not limited to the Department of Labor. During the 1980-1984 period, when outlays for total research rose by more than 40 percent, expenditures for the social sciences were curtailed by about 18 percent. Although federal outlays for all social programs have been increasing rapidly, only 3 percent, or $432 million, was allocated to social science research in 1984.[1] The funding for social research is small in comparison with the cost of supporting the hard sciences and miniscule compared to the cost of operating the government's social programs. The federal government can only assure the nation that it is making a wise investment in social programs if it provides support for a social science research that is commensurate with operating programs.

Policy Recommendations

1. Federal support for ETA's RD&E programs should be expanded, not decreased.

The new Job Training and Partnership Act (JTPA) is experimenting with a new and relatively untested delivery system that places greater emphasis on private-sector initiatives and cooperation in delivering services to economically disadvantaged and displaced workers. The administrators of the JTPA, Congress, and the public need

---

1. Federal support for the social sciences is largely centered in four agencies that provide almost three-fourths of these funds. The 1984 obligations of these agencies were as follows: the Department of Health and Human Services, $142.4 million; the Department of Agriculture, $92.5 million; the Department of Education, $38.4 million; and the National Science Foundation, $34.8 million.

reliable and objective information about this new delivery system. Increased support should be given to social science research and small-scale experimental and development projects so that their findings can help in assessing the effectiveness of the JTPA. The research products of carefully designed experimental projects should raise the level of debate about the usefulness and contributions of employment, training, and other social welfare programs.

2. The National Longitudinal Survey (NLS), a basic national data source that supplies the country with unique information about the labor market experience of our workforce, should be given full and continuous funding.

Longitudinal surveys cannot be subject to inconsistent, intermittent, and inadequate appropriations. Respondents will be lost and the immediacy of the data will not be maintained if long term and sustained funding is not provided.

3. ETA's doctoral dissertation program should be revived and maintained.

The dissertation program has made a major contribution to human resource development by enabling hundreds of young scholars to be trained for work in the field of employment and training. Most of these young professionals have maintained their interest in programs designed to train or retrain economically disadvantaged workers. ETA's relatively small investment in the dissertation program has had a lasting effect on the supply of social researchers from different social science disciplines.

4. The dissemination and utilization of RD&E findings based on studies of employment and training programs should be continued and encouraged.

Dissemination and unlimited access to the findings of government-sponsored social research reflect intellectual freedom in a society dedicated to democratic principles.

ETA should revive its dissemination and utilization program so that its RD&E findings will enable policymakers in the executive branch and Congress, as well as the general public, to make informed decisions about employment and training programs.

The acquisition of information about social and economic problems must be a public concern in a democracy. Governments cannot be effective and responsive without knowledge generated by social science research. The findings of social research can illuminate the complex issues facing our society and assist in avoiding some of the consequences of our major economic and social problems.

FOREWORD

In reflecting on the 1960s and 1970s, many researchers have acknowledged the truly dramatic and substantive changes that occurred in American society in regard to the role and status of minorities, women and the disadvantaged. It is not an exaggeration to conclude that the changes constituted a social revolution that has greatly enhanced the American dream of recognizing the dignity and worth of every human being. Central to this set of changes was the recognition that access to the American dream was gained largely through jobs and income as deprived individuals gained the required training and work opportunities.

The federal legislative initiatives of the 1960s included a requirement that research explore in greater depth the problems being addressed and that evaluation be made of the new programs in employment and training. Program demonstrations and experiments were a natural addition to requirements for research and evaluation. Thus, research, demonstration, and evaluation became integral tools for designing new social policy.

The focus of these proceedings is limited to a review of the programs conducted by the Office of Policy, Evaluation and Research in the Department of Labor's Employment and Training Administration. The National Council on Employment Policy, at its January 1984 meetings, devoted the better part of two days to reviewing the past, examining present policy, and developing modest recommendations for present and future policy. The policy statement reflects the thoughts and conclusions of the Council on the contributions of 20 years of research, demonstration, and evaluation efforts of the Employment and Training Administration of the U.S. Department of Labor.

To aid in its review, the Council commissioned four papers by persons who have played central roles in the development and management of the research, demonstration, and evaluation programs. The reflections of Dr. Eli Ginzberg are especially instructive because of his dual role as researcher and adviser to Presidents, Secretaries of Labor, and the Congress over a period of more than three decades. Dr. Ginzberg's paper is a model for all activist scholars who venture to bridge the two worlds of academic scholarship and public policy activism. Dr. Ginzberg examines the research, demonstration, and evaluation contributions to expanding and improving (a) the number and quality of researchers, (b) the data base, and (c) the methodology of research. His central conclusion is that the program was "highly successful" despite the limitations of the academic environment on which it depended for success.

A review of the 20-year period would also be incomplete without a contribution from Dr. Howard Rosen, who was the central figure within the Department of Labor in shaping and managing the research, demonstration, and evaluation program. He argues that the development of a successful research, demonstration, and evaluation program is possible within a mission-oriented agency only if it is able to demonstrate the usefulness of its findings. He further documents his view that, even with modest resources, it is possible to have a major impact upon the interests and work of the social science research community. He also claims that significant policy changes were made in laws, regulations, and the management of programs as a result of the more than 2,000 studies completed with research, demonstration, and evaluation funding.

A paper by Dr. Gary Burtless and Dr. Robert H. Haveman summarizes the lessons learned from three major labor market experimentation programs conducted in the United States. The Seattle-Denver income maintenance experiment tested the impact of a negative income tax plan on the labor market activity of some 4,800 families over a period of three to five years. The National Supported Work Program was designed to provide one year of work experience to persons with severe employment problems. The Employment Opportunity Pilot Project was a guaranteed jobs program to be tested at 14 sites throughout the United States. The authors conclude that while much was learned from the three programs, such experiments may not be the way to demonstrate the usefulness of basic policy proposals.

In the final paper in this volume, Dr. Daniel Saks suggests a research agenda for employment and training policy in the 1980s. He notes the recent decline in funding for research and focuses attention on issues regarding the organization and administration of a research program.

Collectively these papers and the policy statement provide a much needed review of what has gone on over the past 20 years in employment and training research. It is hoped that the volume will stimulate and encourage research, demonstration, and program evaluation efforts in the future. For some observers of the current scene, the success of the social revolution of the 1960s and 1970s in expanding employment opportunities for minorities, women, and the disadvantaged is by no means complete. While research, demonstration, and evaluation have made an enormous contribution to knowledge and policy, the task, the challenge, and the opportunity continue even though federal financial support is dwindling to the point where the existence of a meaningful program is in doubt.

R. Thayne Robson, *Chairman*
National Council on Employment Policy

Contents

Expanding the Knowledge Base for Informed Public Policy

The U.S. Department of Labor's Research Program 1963-1978*

Eli Ginzberg

1. Introduction

When asked to take on this assignment, I immediately responded in the affirmative since my colleagues and I at the Conservation of Human Resources (CHR), Columbia University, have been major beneficiaries of DOL funding throughout the two decades. Clearly our beneficiary status necessitates that this special relationship be acknowledged, but it did not justify my turning down the invitation. Except for the most recent generation of manpower researchers, all who have worked in the field of human resources and manpower had been beneficiaries of DOL, some more, some less.

*Anna Dutka, a long-time member of the Conservation staff who has assisted me on many earlier projects, was most helpful on the present assignment. She found many of the critical items that I have reviewed; she checked a great many details with informed persons inside and outside of the federal government; she made sure that text and footnotes were aligned; and she took over responsibility of turning my draft manuscript into final product. For all of this assistance, and more, I am deeply in her debt.

1

My solution to this conflict of interest is relatively simple: I will not deal with the multiple research products that the Conservation of Human Resources produced beyond calling the reader's attention to the brief descriptive summary that can be found in *Research and Development: A 16-Year Compendium (1963-78)* (hereinafter cited as *Compendium); The Conservation of Human Resources Project: Fortieth Anniversary Report,* Columbia University, March 1979; and a listing and brief notation of the principal CHR research supported by DOL appended to this paper.

Let me further note that because of various governmental and nongovernmental positions, I had other interlocking relationships with the Department of Labor's Office of Research and Development (ORD), in particular, as Chairman, National Commission for Employment Policy and as Chairman of the Board, Manpower Demonstration and Research Corporation.

The above helps to make the record clear. But I should also add that I have had a long and close friendship with Howard Rosen, the long term director of ORD.

2. Orientation

The above potential sources of conflicts of interest having been specified, it is desirable, if not essential, that I touch at least briefly on a number of intellectual and emotional predispositions that have long helped to shape my thinking about research in human resources and manpower as well as in the broader arena of social investigations.

As a pupil of Wesley Clair Mitchell and John Maurice Clark, I come out of the "institutional school of economics" with deep skepticism about the applicability of mainline economics as an explanatory theory of the U.S. and world economies. My skepticism has been that much greater when it comes to applying neoclassical economics to the analysis of human resources and the labor market.[1]

Further, I am in fundamental disagreement with the positivistic tradition of the Chicago School, which believes that economics is a "value-free" discipline and that the results of the researcher are totally independent of his political orientation. Aristotle taught that man is a political animal. Hence he can engage in value-free social inquiries only if he were able to think and reflect outside of his own skin. But I cannot conceive of such a disembodied researcher.[2]

Let me call attention to a few more preconceptions and prejudices. While money, especially large amounts of money, can, over a period of years, alter a research environment by increasing the number of trained researchers, a significant transformation requires considerable time. Even when successful, as in the case of biomedical research which saw federal expenditures increase from about $65 million in 1950 to about $4 billion in 1984, the much enlarged research establishment may make very slow progress in solving complex problems such as understanding the causative factors in cancer.

Further, the institutional reinforcement that established doctrines and techniques receive from the academic leadership does not yield ground readily—not even in the presence of new, large, and sustained research and development expenditures. The reasons are not difficult to appreciate: most good researchers are interested in an academic career and have the best prospects of success if they conform at least to the extent where their seniors and peers publish their articles and vote to grant them tenure.

Reformulated, the foregoing implies that a federal research and development program is inevitably and to a large degree the captive of the academic establishment.

Many will say this is as it should be; but moral imperatives aside, this is how it has been and will probably long continue to be.

Federal research funds are made available by Congress with the Administration playing a leading or, at a minimum, a supporting role. Hence there is no possible way for a federal research and development program to get under way and flourish unless those concerned with its growth and well-being keep, at all times, not one but two ears to the ground. Skillful research administrators must make a large number of compromises on both the administrative and the legislative fronts if a continuing dollar flow is to be secured. They are most successful if they know where they want to go and succeed in moving ahead with only an occasional detour.

Finally, one must recognize that the most important advances in the natural and the social sciences are the work of men of genius.[3] By definition, not even the best planned, financed and executed research and development program has learned how to increase the number of geniuses. All that it can accomplish is to improve the methods, the data, the personnel and the environment which may sooner or later lead to a major breakthrough that will advance the discipline.

3. Criteria and Overview

The results of an assessment of a research and development program depend on the criteria employed. If the criterion is a major intellectual breakthrough, the odds are overwhelming, for the reasons just adumbrated, that the evaluation will be negative.

What other, more reasonable criteria, might be used to assess a research and development program? Three have already been alluded to in passing: the enlargement of the research pool, the improvement in the data base, and the development of new, as well as the reinforcement of existing, methodologies. In the assessment that follows, we will start by making use of each of these three criteria.

One can begin this assessment by noting that ORD, through its dissertational grant program,[4] enlarged the pool of young researchers by an order of magnitude. During the 16-year period under review, it added almost 500 new doctorates to the pool.

A second major accomplishment of ORD was its significant strengthening of the data base. Most of the 2000 or so grants and contracts which it funded yielded some new data about some facet or facets of the labor market. But ORD made its largest single commitment, beginning in 1965, to improve the data base by funding the National Longitudinal Surveys at Ohio State.

On the third front, the development of new methodology, ORD moved circumspectly. It was cognizant of a division of labor between itself and the National Science Foundation, whose charter gave the latter more scope to support research aimed at the development and refinement of theories and techniques. On the other hand, Congress encouraged ORD to undertake evaluative studies of manpower programs and in the process considerable advances in evaluation techniques were achieved. One must add, however, that many evaluations contributed little if anything to improved results, substantive or methodological.

The single most useful volume that deals with the ORD program is a collection of papers contributed by Ray Marshall, Denis Johnston, Michael Piore, Glen Cain, Peter Barth, Vernon Briggs and Herbert Parnes under the editorship of Gordon Swanson and Jon Michaelson.[5] These papers were prepared for the Committee on Department of Labor Manpower Research and Development of the National

Academy of Science, chaired by Gordon Swanson, that had undertaken a review of the ORD program and published its report in the mid-1970s under the title *Knowledge and Policy in Manpower.*[6]

Peter Barth, in his contributed paper, calls attention to several ways in which a review of research can be approached: concentration on the subject areas that have received attention; assessment of the quality of the research; determination of the existence of patterns; evaluation of the timeliness of the research and its relevance to policy formulation; the cost/benefit ratio involved; and finally, the possibilities for improvement.[7]

There is surely nothing wrong with the above listing and Barth recognized that additional criteria could easily be added. From among this large number I will select only two to add to the three criteria noted earlier for the purposes of this assessment—the quality of the research and its contribution to program development and policy.

A first approximation suggests that many of the 2000 projects were of good quality—the subject was sensible, the data collection and the analyses were carried out in a workmanlike fashion, and the findings made some contribution to the program or policy. The best among them made multiple contributions.

With respect to the relation of ORD results to public policy, a presumptive conclusion is that Congress must have given the program at least a passing mark because of its willingness to keep funding it.

By way of recapitulation, the following five criteria have been identified as central to the assessment to which this paper is dedicated:

— The enlargement of the research pool.
— The improvement of the data base.

— The development of new methodology.
— The quality of the research projects.
— The contribution to public policy.

4. Labor Economics: A Longer View

By way of setting it is important, especially for the orientation of the younger members of the profession, to call attention to the state of "labor economics" (to use the most inclusive term that was earlier in vogue) that distinguished the American academic scene prior to the passage of the Manpower Development and Training Act in 1962.

What follows is based largely on memory and personal experience, sharpened by a rereading of the materials referred to in this assessment. It also clearly shows some of my prejudices and preferences.

The leaders of labor economics in the 1950s—John Dunlop, Charles Myers, Frederick Harbison, and Clark Kerr, the first three of whom were charter members of the National Council for Employment Policy and also served as chairmen of the Council in its formative years—were busy studying the impact of industrialization on labor, primarily in the developing nations. Without resorting to psychohistory, a reasonable presumption is that they found overseas a more exciting research arena than the United States during the Eisenhower era of goodwill during which management and unions were getting along and the problems of the poor, the blacks, and women had not yet risen to a high level of consciousness.

In the mid-1950s, when the National Manpower Council put the subject of "womanpower" on its agenda of possible areas for future investigation, the vote in favor of pursuing the inquiry passed by a single vote! When the final report *Womanpower*[8] was presented to President Eisenhower he remarked: "Oh yes, women were very important in the European Theater of Operations; they did very good work as telephone operators, chauffeurs, and nurses"!

At about the same time, one of the more literate members of the New York banking community was unable to comprehend what was meant by the term "human resources" until he was informed that it was a broader term for the arena usually subsumed under military and civilian manpower. In fact, when Frederick Harbison relocated from the University of Chicago to Princeton he made a detour via New York to learn about the range of subjects that the Conservation of Human Resources Project at Columbia was working on.

In late 1953, shortly after James P. Mitchell, one of my favorites among the sixteen Secretaries of Labor with whom I have consulted, as appointed, he designated an informal 5-man advisory committee to assist him in reorienting the Department of Labor. Douglas V. Brown of Princeton served as informal chairman and Kerr and I were members, together with Cy Ching and a Washington consultant. Our principal recommendation was that the Department of Labor should become the manpower agency of the federal government. Mitchell was comfortable with this recommendation but there was very little that he could do in the 1950s to implement it.

Two more observations. The majority of academicians interested in labor economics were based at, or closely aligned with, industrial relations institutions located at a few of the major private universities but primarily at the principal state universities of which Cornell, Michigan, Michigan State, Illinois, Minnesota, and California, both at Berkeley and at Los Angeles, were among the leaders.

An inspection of the contents of the *Industrial and Labor Relations Review* in the early 1960s discloses that most of the issue was given over to a symposium on "Industrial Relations in Latin America."[9] The other three principal articles dealt with "Fringe Benefits and Overtime as Barriers to Expanding Employment," "Labor Relations in the Postal Service" and "The Relation of the Labor Force to Employment." None of the articles made use of a single regression; they relied on descriptive statistics—nothing more.

Much the same was true for the first issue of the *Journal of Human Resources* which appeared in the summer of 1966.[10] Of the five principal articles on investing in human capital, the supply of and demand for college teachers, occupational data requirements for education planning, the effects of general education on manpower programs, and the economics of health, education and welfare, not one made use of econometrics or mathematical modeling.

So much for the status of labor economics in academe at the onset of ORD. How did the breakthrough in federal manpower policy, including research funding, occur? The successful political initiative owed much to the work and findings of two committees in the House and the Senate under Representative Elmer Holland and Senator Joseph Clark, both of Pennsylvania, during 1960 and 1961. The committee hearings called attention to the growing incidence and prevalence of unemployment. Curtis Aller and Garth Mangum did yeoman service as staff directors of the House and Senate committees, respectively. It is worth recalling that the Republicans played a major role in passing the MDTA legislation.

Further, Senator Paul Douglas of Illinois had worked long and hard to obtain federal assistance for depressed areas and the Area Redevelopment Act was finally passed and signed in 1961 by President Kennedy.

Senator Clark, shortly after the election of President Kennedy, asked me to assemble a group of academicians and other experts for a meeting with him at the Harvard Club in New York City to explore a Congressional manpower initiative. Arthur Goldberg was one of the invitees, but had to cancel at the last moment because the President announced his appointment as Secretary of Labor. Among the major recommendations that the group made to Senator Clark was to include in any new legislation a requirement that the President submit an annual report on manpower to the Congress which would help to focus the attention of the nation on the subject. Further, the group recommended Congress provide funding for a research and development program.

One more piece of history. Seymour Wolfbein who had been assigned by Secretary Mitchell and reassigned by Secretary Goldberg a leading role in the Department of Labor's emerging manpower efforts, asked me to talk with the Secretary while the Manpower Development and Training bill was making its way through Congress about the need for a job creation program to accompany a job training program. The Secretary heard me out, indicated that he agreed, but added that the White House would go for a modest training bill and nothing more.

5. Assessment

The basis for the appraisals offered below requires clarification. I did not read, much less study with care, the 2000 or so completed research investigations. Some of the reports emerging from the more important research efforts were known to me since they first were made public and I have sought to refresh my memory about those that I considered relevant for the present exercise. Further, I turned the pages and read most of the text in the *Compendium* and reviewed with some care the two publications of the National Academy of Sciences. As noted earlier, I also did some sampling of the journals to refresh my memory of their scope and coverage at the beginning and end of the period under consideration.

With this preamble, the assessment of ORD's program in terms of the five criteria that were earlier identified can proceed.

The Enlargement of the Research Pool

There is good reason to believe that in the absence of ORD's liberal funding for manpower studies, the principal centers of research in labor economics—the industrial relations centers identified above—would have continued surely for a long time in their accustomed ways, allocating most of their resources to problems of collective bargaining and closely related issues. In fact, even in the presence of multiple sources of funding, including not only ORD but also other federal agencies such as the National Science Foundation, National Institutes of Health, and the Departments of Commerce and HEW, to note only the more important, the industrial relations centers moved slowly and haltingly to shift the focus of their research interests towards human resources and manpower. A few moved energetically, but most took only small steps.

ORD, faced with this relatively inflexible research structure, moved to institution building, part of the aim of which was to strengthen the research pool by making a series of "institutional grants."[11] Most of the grants were funded for a period of between four and five years with a total of four rounds of awards between 1966 and 1978.[12] The funds provided for modest staff expansion, some scholarships, curriculum building, and some research support. The last two rounds shifted the program's focus from teaching and research to professional training for CETA staff in the several regions of the country.

A total of just under 50 institutional grants were made. An early and continuing target was to assist the curricula development of minority-based colleges and universities so that they could provide broadened opportunities for their students to qualify for careers in employment and training.[13] An inspection of the list of grantee institutions suggests that, aside from the considerable number of minority-based institutions, about ten to a dozen represented universities that had demonstrated a sustained high level of research capability in labor economics and/or employment and training.

By far the most exciting undertaking in the arena of research resource development was the Doctoral Dissertation Grants program. Almost 500 of these, completed and in process, are listed in the *Compendium*.[14] Three publications prepared by Lawrence Klein, formerly of the Department of Labor, who relocated to the University of Arizona, provide a window into those dissertations that were judged to have the most merit in terms of the quality of the research and the relevance of the findings.[15]

Among the unique characteristics of the dissertational support program was the fact that ORD encouraged students from all of the social sciences to apply, and that the selection committee of outside experts responded by allocating roughly one-half of the grants to economists and the balance to other social scientists from anthropology to demography.

The best way to indicate the quality of the grantees is to list those with whose work I am reasonably well acquainted who appear on the first 14 pages (10 percent) of the total listing: Lawrence S. Seidman, Gilbert Cardenas, Gregory DeFreitas, Lionel J. Hausman, Marjorie H. Honig, Michael Boskin, Robert D. Reischauer, Jonathan R. Kesselman, Robert J. Flanagan, Stephan T. Marston, Harvey S. Rosen. If the foregoing ratio were to hold throughout, it would mean that this one appraiser would have a more or less intimate acquaintance with the work of about one-fifth of the entire group—no small visibility considering that a considerable number of researchers at the time that the *Compendium* was published had not yet completed their projects.

Faced with a gross shortage of manpower researchers, ORD responded quickly and with imagination to remedy this most serious of bottlenecks. By establishing the Doctoral Dissertational Grants program in 1965 and by opening it up to all social science students who had completed their work for a doctorate, other than writing their dissertation, ORD made a major contribution by both attracting high talent into the manpower arena and at the same time broadening the boundaries of the field by encouraging applicants from all of the social sciences.

The Institutional Grants program was more of a mixed bag, largely because of strong pressure from the policymakers to direct much or most of the money to objectives other than the advancement of manpower research. I don't want to convey the impression that the institutional grants made no contribution to the furtherance of research, only that their contribution was relatively minor. It should also be noted that ORD, had it been free to design the program according to its own preferences, would probably have spent a large proportion of the total funds at the nation's strongest academic centers with a demonstrated capability to undertake significant manpower research. But that option was not available.

Improving the Data Base

This is the second criterion that we earlier identified to guide us in this appraisal of ORD's program. As Clark Kerr recently remarked in "The Intellectual Role of the Neorealists in Labor Economics," one of the long-term contributions of those who focused their attention on the operations of labor and labor markets has been to improve and correct the faulty assumptions and conclusions of the economic theorists about how labor markets operate.[16] In fact Wassily Leontief, in his sharp and insightful presidential address to the American Economic Association, took note of the continuing misallocation of the resources between data gathering and model construction with the disproportionate emphasis on the latter.[17]

In the mid-1960s, when Daniel Patrick Moynihan was Assistant Secretary of Labor, he and the director of ORD took the initiative to devote a considerable proportion of the then quite modest research budget into a long term effort to improve the data base by funding the National Longitudinal Surveys of Labor Force Behavior (NLS) at The Ohio State University under the leadership of Professor Herbert S. Parnes in association with the Demographic Survey Division of the Bureau of the Census.

The NLS study has focused attention on four groups—older men, middle-aged women, and young people, both male and female. In 1979 it added a new and enlarged youth cohort. Its informational net has been cast wide to include a host of variables, including economic, sociological and psychological, in order to permit study of the interactions among the principal forces that determine outcomes of different groups in the labor market. The NLS deliberately oversampled for minorities. From the outset, a unique aspect of the surveys was the frequent reinterviewing of the same individuals.

The *Compendium* lists the large number of studies of labor force behavior that derive directly from the NLS.[18] In her assessment of the NLS, June O'Neill of the Urban Institute singled out for special attention three research areas where the Surveys yielded much valuable new insight: Unemployment and Related Labor Market Issues; Women's Labor Force Participation and Male-Female Earnings Differentials; and Aging and the Retired.[19]

While Parnes and his many associates at Ohio State took the lead in analyzing the rich materials that the Sureys were yielding, ORD arranged along the line that the research community would have easy and low cost access to the tapes. Once again, I resorted to a sampling approach to call attention to some of the analysts who, under ORD grants, made use of the Survey data: D.H. Nafziger, J.L. Holland, Robert E. Hall, Jacob Mincer, Herman P. Miller, Robert J. Flanagan, Ernst Stromsdorfer.[20]

Those wise in the ways of the Washington bureaucracy and the halls of Congress will appreciate that the launching of the NLS was not easy. There is always a strong resistance to spending governmental funds on data collection. But even more difficult is to keep a project such as the NLS going. Next year will mark its twentieth birthday, a remarkably long life for such an effort. As the editors of *Manpower Research and Labor Economics* remarked in their introductory note to Herbert Parnes' article: "The National Longitudinal Surveys (NLS) constitute a unique research effort in the manpower field; indeed this study is a landmark in the social sciences as a whole during the past decade."[21] Parnes, with his customary modesty, concluded his interim assessment with the comment, "There is, of course, no way of determining whether the National Longitudinal Surveys have been worth the millions of dollars they have cost."[22]

Under the single heading of "Labor Demand," the *Compendium* lists over 100 projects that ORD funded, many of which had as their primary or secondary aim the improvement of the data base.[23] While no one project, nor possibly the entire group, can approach the NLS, they underscore the sensitivity of ORD to improving the data sources available to researchers. In this connection, one must not overlook the useful appendices prepared by ORD that appear at the end of the annual *Manpower Report of the President,* later renamed the *Employment and Training Report of the President.* The tables therein reproduced and brought up to date every year have undoubtedly saved researchers untold hours in gaining access to current data on which they depend so heavily.

The Development of New Methodology

As noted in section 3, when this subject was first addressed, ORD sought not to get too involved in funding projects the principal aim of which was to develop new methodology. Despite its self-imposed restraint, one can still identify a commendable contribution that ORD made to the improvement of methodology even though such gains were often closely related to data improvement, program design and policy clarification. In the Index of Research Subjects in the *Compendium* one finds about 50 titles under "Methodology" including the following important areas: accuracy in manpower projections; America's uncounted people; cost-benefit analysis of manpower programs; income dynamics of the poor; internal labor markets; job vacancies in the firm and the labor market; methods of forecasting short-term unemployment change; occupations—meanings and measures; short-term manpower projection methods; and working life tables for the U.S.[24] This one listing under "Methodology" in no way provides an overview of the full scope of ORD's efforts in this area. About the same number of titles are found under "Assessment and Evaluation."

Once again, a useful approach to the quality of these investigations is suggested by noting the names of some of the researchers and the investigations that they pursued: Robert E. Hall explored the Keynesian dichotomy between frictional and involuntary unemployment in periods of full employment;[25] R.A. Gordon, Michael L. Wachter and Karl E. Taeuber prepared papers on demographic trends and full employment;[26] Michael J. Boskin explored a model of occupational choice based on the theory of human capital and estimated by conditional logit analysis;[27] Charles C. Holt and his associates at the Urban Institute carried on extensive studies of job search and labor turnover dynamics in order to gain a better understanding of employment in an inflationary era;[28] Richard A. Easterlin studied long swings in labor force growth;[29] Stanley Lebergott sought to develop new methods of forecasting short term unemployment changes;[30] James G. Scoville addressed conceptual and measurement problems in occupational analyses;[31] and Orley Ashenfelter investigated the use of various econometric models to assess the impacts of training.[32]

Imbedded in sections 1 and 2 of the *Compendium* one finds methodological contributions from other leading economists and social scientists including: Finis Welch and Marvin Kosters; Laurits R. Christensen and Dale N. Jorgensen; Lawrence R. Klein; Phoebus Dhrymes; Lester C. Thurow; Edward D. Kalachek and many more with a national and international reputation.[33]

By far the largest single financial commitment of ORD to the improvement of methodology was its liberal multiyear funding of the Manpower Research and Demonstration Corporation evaluation effort carried out under the title of "Supported Work," with Mathematica as the prime contractor and the Poverty Institute at the University of Wisconsin as the major subcontractor. The cost of the research, which was based on random assignment of clients with experimental and control groups and involved baseline interviews and multiyear follow-up interviews, approximated 11 million dollars.[34]

ORD was distressed that with so many billions being invested in training programs, definitive answers as to whether or not they made a difference in terms of postemployment and earnings experience were hard to produce. Moreover, it was even more uncertain whether such programs could help the most disadvantaged groups in the population. Hence its willingness to spend a large sum on a well-designed research design that would be properly implemented and where the results could command respect.

The results turned out to be mixed: the AFDC mothers group definitely showed large benefits from work; the results for the ex-addicts were equivocal; and there were no gains for the ex-offenders and youth. I was restive from the outset about the high cost of this evaluation but my colleagues convinced me of the value of a scientific evaluation. I also recall Robert Lampman's warning that the null hypothesis would probably be sustained.

Before concluding this section on methodology, I would like to add a few observations. I believe that ORD was correct in not undertaking heavy financing of methodological inquiries. Had it done so, the odds are strong that it would have added substantially to its ongoing difficulties of sustaining support for its research program both within the Department of Labor and in the Congress. Further I suspect that many of the most important methodological advances in the manpower arena, as in other fields of inquiry, are often the by-products of investigations directed at substantive goals.

It made sense for both the Congress and the Administration to become interested in evaluating the results of various programmatic interventions to assist the unemployed and other disadvantaged groups. But this belated interest, which blossomed with the passage of CETA in 1973, led to the explosive growth of for-profit firms, many of which were located in the Washington area, which became highly adept at pressuring the various federal agencies, including the Department of Labor, for evaluation contracts. For the most part, the programs had not been designed and implemented in terms of participant selection, data collection, controls, output measures and follow-up to yield meaningful results when formal evaluation techniques were applied. As sections 4D and 4E in the *Compendium* make clear, ORD was successful through 1978 in not bending very far in the direction of this new enthusiasm.[35] When the new Administration came into office in 1981, however, evaluations became a favorite of the policymakers in the Department of Labor.

One of the opportunities for learning more about the participants of various training programs that in my view was largely neglected was to tap into Social Security records for follow-up information. Admittedly, access to Social Security records is hard to come by, especially for research purposes; the matching process is difficult and the limited amount of follow-up information will constrain what can be learned. Still, it represents perhaps the least expensive way to get a fast reading on the effectiveness of large public investments in employment and training programs.

My direct experience with specially designed evaluation programs such as "Supported Work" has impressed me with their cost. On the other hand, attempts to economize, as in the case of the Youth Entitlement Program (Manpower Research and Development Corporation and Abt Associates), by reliance on a matching of so-called "comparable cities" such as Baltimore and Cleveland, can turn out to have many disadvantages.

The Quality of the Research Projects

If one were to single out just one, rather than five criteria with which to assess ORD's program, my preference would be to use "the quality of the research projects." As I have indicated earlier, good research in the social arena will, more often than not, have a policy orientation and in the process the researcher will often contribute to enlarging the data base and score an advance over existing methodology. Accordingly, many of the projects that are referred to below, as well as many previously discussed, could without distortion be placed in other categories since as with all systems of categorization, but particularly with the one that we are following, a large element of arbitrariness cannot be avoided.

About half of the pages of the *Compendium* are directed to listing and briefly discussing the research projects under two principal headings: 1. The Economics, Social and Policy Background; and 2. The Labor Market. Sections 3 and 4 deal more specifically with training and administration. In the pages that follow I will comment solely on research projects listed in sections 1 and 2.

There is no possible way for me, without excessive elaboration, to take note of all the research work that warrants attention because the investigator addressed an important subject; he or she dealt with it according to accepted research canons, and the results make a contribution both to the pool of knowledge and to public policy.

My selections aim rather to provide the reader an overview of the range of support that ORD provided and the important subjects that the research illuminated. In the very first year, 1963, Margaret S. Gordon studied the European experience with employment and training, thereby providing U.S. officials with a road map.[36] Benjamin Shimberg and his colleagues undertook pioneering work in the arena of occupational licensing.[37] David S. North and Marion F. Houstoun produced an important exploratory study of the characteristics and role of illegal aliens in the U.S. labor market.[38] Frank Levy and his colleagues Clair B. Vickery and Michael L. Wiseman contributed significant new knowledge and understanding to the income dynamics of the poor.[39]

Lester C. Thurow's book on *Generating Inequality* was the outgrowth of a research project in which he explored the concept of job competition in contrast to the neoclassical wage competition model of the labor market.[40]

The final stage of T. Aldrich Finegan's and William G. Bowen's classic study of labor force participation rates was supported by ORD.[41]

Richard B. Freeman's basic research on engineers and scientists in an industrial economy which led to his well-known work, *The Overeducated American,* grew out of ORD support.[42]

John T. Dunlop and Daniel Quinn Mills had a series of grants which enabled them to assess in depth the changing capacity of the construction industry to adapt to changing labor requirements and to modify their training systems accordingly.[43]

Louis E. Davis of the University of California, Los Angeles, the father of the Quality of Work Life in the United States, received early support from ORD which also provided considerable support for the Human Interaction Research Institute (Los Angeles) as well as for the work of Stanley Seashore and his colleagues at the Survey Research Center at the University of Michigan, all of which resulted in a considerable number of interesting publications.[44]

Sheppard and Belitsky's study, *The Job Hunt,* published in the mid-1960s represented a departure. They explored more broadly than earlier researchers the motivational and attitudinal dimensions via a case approach of how unemployed workers look for jobs.[45] This effort reaffirmed the wisdom of ORD's broader approach to labor market processes than was characteristic of most economists.

A quite different approach, more ambitious and with more far-reaching results, was carried out over a five-year period (1968-73) by F. Ray Marshall of the University of Texas at Austin in his study *Negro Employment in the South.* Six southern cities were the focus of this inquiry: Atlanta, Birmingham, Houston, Louisville, Memphis and Miami. Important findings emerged from analysis of the factors that contributed to a lowering of the barriers against black workers. At the same time, the research pointed to major difficulties that continued to handicap blacks both at the point of being hired and also in advancing up the job ladder.[46]

Cynthia Fuchs Epstein of Columbia University explored the factors that hinder or facilitate women's entrance into such prestigious professions as law, medicine, science, and academe. The author noted that the early socialization process of girls and young women as well as later institutionalized barriers acted to reduce the potential supply. Her analysis and findings led to a major book entitled *Women's Place: Options and Limits in Professional Careers.*[47]

The foregoing selections are illustrative of the large number of important research projects supported by ORD which covered a wide range of critical policy areas and yielded important new knowledge about the operations of the labor market. The outstanding accomplishment of the research program, surely in terms of intellectual impact and long term influence, was the work of Peter B. Doeringer and Michael Piore, *Internal Labor Markets and Manpower Analysis,* which was started in 1966 and completed in 1970.[48]

The data that the authors used to study the operations of manufacturing firms in adjusting to imbalances in labor supply and technological changes were derived from an earlier project that had also been funded by ORD. The authors stressed the dynamics of freedom that medium-sized and large employers have and exercise in making adjustments in their labor supply through hiring, screening, training, recruitment, and subcontracting, relying on these approaches much more than on wage adjustments to assure themselves of the range of workers and skills that they require.

The authors also concluded that disadvantaged members of the labor force, minorities and women, found it very difficult to break into the sector of stable, internal labor markets and were therefore crowded into the "secondary" labor market characterized by short term, low-skill, low-paying jobs which in turn had a major impact on the ways in which such disadvantaged groups adjust to work and life. The authors concluded that these disadvantaged groups live on the periphery of the labor market and society and have little opportunity to join the mainstream. Hence the term, "the dual labor market."

In the Brookings Papers, Michael L. Wachter undertook a 43-page critique of what he subtitled the "Dual Approach," which was followed by comments and discussion including remarks by Piore.[49] In Wachter's analysis, the dual labor market approach is predicted on the following: differences in firm behavior in the high and low wage sectors; a distinction between good and bad jobs, not between skilled and unskilled workers; and movement of workers in the secondary labor market among low wage jobs and between unemployment and labor force participation.

Wachter concluded that it is wrong to assume that the internal labor market in the primary sector does not follow the employer's search for efficiency and that it is wrong to differentiate sharply between the primary and secondary markets since mobility exists between them. Further, pervasive underemployment need not be the key characteristic of the secondary labor market. But Wachter is not all negative: he believes that the dual labor market theorists have made significant contributions in focusing on wage-setting behavior in the secondary market; in introducing feedback effects into their model; and in deepening understanding of the unemployment mechanism. Each is important and the three together represent a major advance.

In a recent contribution to the *Discussion Paper Series* of the Harvard Institute of Economic Research, "Troubled Workers in the Labor Market," Richard B. Freeman concludes his review of the dual labor market hypothesis with the following comment: "In short, the dual market claim regarding wage determination processes appears to be valid, but its other assertions have yet to be shown to be empirically correct."[50] This is no small praise for a theory 14 years after it was first introduced and after it has been subjected to repeated and detailed critiques.

The ORD record of quality research projects would have to be assessed as respectable, if not outstanding, even without the Doeringer-Piore contribution. But its rating must be raised once one takes cognizance of the fact that it subsidized one of the few intellectual breakthroughs in the conceptualization of labor markets in the decades of the 1960s and 1970s.

Contributions to Public Policy

Although we have noted in passing that many of the projects previously identified have had a direct or indirect impact on manpower programs and policies, the investigations reviewed below have been selected specifically to emphasize this facet of ORD's total effort. The projects have been selected with an eye to illustrating the impact of ORD's projects on broad manpower policy as well as on specific programmatic improvements. Some fall in the zone between the two.

As far as broad policy considerations are concerned, one can identify projects that encouraged Congress to adopt new or more expansive stances with respect to public service employment, extended unemployment insurance, work-fare, improved articulation between remedial education and skill training, mobility allowances and upgrading efforts.

The research program also had significant beneficial effects on expanding apprenticeship opportunities for black men, on placing black women in the South in white-collar and technical positions with career opportunities, in helping ex-offenders to gain a permanent attachment to the labor market, in helping persuade the courts to permit young people awaiting trial to participate in supervised work programs, in persuading the Department of Defense to modify its selection criteria so that a quarter of a million who, under previous standards, would have been rejected were accepted.

The following pages provide some elaboration of the foregoing. In the early 1970s, a series of University of California-based investigations focused on the Bay Area, including one by Robert A. Gordon and Lloyd Ulman, concluded that public service employment could be increased by 10 to 15 percent in low-skilled categories without severe disruption or costly new inputs.[51] Later in the decade, the Urban Institute in Washington, under the direction of Lee Bawden, concluded that opportunities existed for 3 million public sector jobs in 21 program areas.[52] In the late 1960s and early 1970s, two ORD contracts with the National Civil Service League led to an estimate, based on summary data, that more than 400,000 yearly vacancies were available in state and local governments for the employment of disadvantaged workers.[53]

The foregoing, together with additional projects outlined in the *Compendium* under section 3G, "Providing Public Employment,"[54] surely contributed to the decision of President Carter to request, and Congress to agree to, a vast increase in PSE jobs in the latter years of the 1970s.

The carefully crafted and carried out study of unemployment insurance exhaustees by Mathematica in 1974-76[55] concluded, among other findings, that UI did not operate as a serious work disincentive and that even among many who withdrew from the labor force after their benefits were exhausted, a significant proportion wanted to return to employment. These findings, among others, surely reinforced the subsequent actions of the Congress to extend the periods of coverage, even in the face of budgetary stringencies and the opposition of an Administration that sought to reduce income transfer payments.

The Minnesota Work Equity Program, which got under way in 1977, sought to test an alternative to income transfers for welfare clients by providing guaranteed work or training as alternatives. The principal components were an expansion of public service jobs at or near the minimum wage, expanded training opportunities on the job or in the classroom, and placement of 10 percent of the clients into unsubsidized jobs. The lessons learned from this undertaking, evaluated by Abt Associates, surely encouraged President Reagan and the Congress to modify existing welfare legislation to encourage the states to experiment with work-fare.[56] Even without the benefit of any specific research findings, the Department of Labor early recognized (1963) that MDTA had to be amended to enable many of the unemployed to undergo a remedial educational experience before entering upon occupational training. If my memory is correct, the Director of ORD was alerted to this need on the basis of his trips to the field during the early months of the training program. In any event, the Congress agreed with this assessment.

The most successful linkage between remedial education and skill training occurred at Job Corps Centers, but only a small number of disadvantaged youth profited from the experience. In 1977, Congress, in passing the Youth Employment and Training Program, specifically reserved some part of the total funds, 22 percent, for use by the educational authorities to encourage them to improve their efforts at remedial instruction, especially for out-of-school youth who were returning to school to take advantage of the program. ORD did not make more than an occasional grant for remedial education. Again, if my memory serves me correctly, this was viewed as the domaim of HEW.

In the case of "Facilitating Geographic Mobility," the Congress acted first (1965), directing the Department of Labor to mount efforts to assist unemployed and underemployed workers to relocate to areas where there are more and better jobs available.

Demonstration mobility projects were launched in 28 states and a total of 14,000 workers were relocated.[57] The Employment Service undertook a major 3-year effort, beginning in 1969, to assist farm migrants based in South Texas to settle out of the migrating stream. Abt Associates undertook the assessment and published a 4-volume report.[58]

The relatively modest number of workers who were successfully relocated (many who made a successful move later returned home) and the formidable difficulties encountered in diverting settlement out of the migrating stream appeared to me at the time, and also now in retrospect, to explain why Congress never moved in a big way to subsidize worker mobility. Politics was an additional barrier. Congressmen from counties losing population do not readily vote funds to speed the outmigration of their constituents. The equivocal results from the demonstrations strengthened their opposition.

ORD, through contacts with Mobilization for Youth and Howard University in 1965 and 1966, focused on preparing disadvantaged youth for entrance into paraprofessional occupations with focus on jobs in health care. These early efforts provided a favorable backdrop to Congressional action in 1967 when it passed the New Careers amendment. Thereafter ORD expanded its upgrading demonstration efforts in all three sectors of the economy—private, nonprofit, government.[59] Among the most interesting and rewarding was its decade-long effort at the U.S. Atomic Energy Commission plants at Oak Ridge where it succeeded in moving a considerable number of poorly educated local persons into skilled and technical jobs through carefully structured learning and on-the-job experiences.[60]

The foregoing illustrations of the interface between ORD's projects and Congressional action do not "prove" that without the former, legislative action would not have occurred. All that this suggests is the probability of ORD's influence, both positive and occasionally negative (mobility), on Congressional action.

There is a presumption in the United States that the measure of influence on public policy is best revealed by Congressional action to pass new laws and make new appropriations since by such actions Congress can affect all or a large part of the entire population. But clearly, as noted below, ORD had considerable policy impact other than through persuading Congress to act. We will inspect five more striking success stories.

F. Ray Marshall and Vernon M. Briggs, Jr. undertook in 1966 and completed the following year a study of 10 major cities with large black populations aimed at assessing the barriers blocking the entrance of blacks into apprenticeship. The more important recommendations emerging from this study are set out in the *Compendium's* abstract.[61] The critical point for this assessment is to be read in the striking gains in the numbers of minorities who succeeded in being accepted as trainees in subsequent years and the striking gains in the number of journeymen, at least in some, if not all, unions. Those who followed the lowering of the barriers have no question that the Marshall-Briggs study, *The Negro and Apprenticeships,*[62] served as the wedge that the leadership in both the public and private sectors used to accomplish this striking advance.

The Minority Women Employment Program was another outstandingly successful effort of ORD. Based on an Atlanta pilot study of the early 1970s, the aim of the demonstration was to determine whether a specially targeted outreach effort could place college-educated minority women in nontraditional managerial, professional and technical occupations, primarily in the private sector. In addition to Atlanta, the program became operational in Dallas, New Orleans, Tulsa, Cincinnati and Los Angeles. The major steps in the program were to identify desirable openings, to coach and support likely candidates to increase their prospects of being hired and then to help them to retain their jobs. By 1978, five years into the program, over 1300 women had been placed, with many of them representing the first minority women ever hired into these higher level positions.[63]

Starting in the very first year of MDTA, ORD focused considerable effort and resources in assisting prisoners and ex-offenders through a series of imaginative and often difficult and risky demonstrations. These involved gaining approval of the prison authorities to provide training for inmates by taking advantage of the 1966 amendments to MDTA which no longer limited eligible trainees to persons in the labor force. In the late 1960s, ORD funding enabled the Vera Institute in New York City to undertake two pioneering projects using pretrial interventions to provide persons under arrest and awaiting trial with training and employment opportunities. If the trainee's performance warranted, the project staff recommended dismissal of the charges.[64]

Still another, relatively late, effort was to provide transitional financial aid to newly released prisoners to assist them in making it back in civilian society and into the world of work. At the time when the *Compendium* was being published ORD had achieved some successes together, as one might have anticipated, with some failures. But it must not be overlooked that the resources available to ORD to help this large population were quite limited.

The last impact study goes back to the earliest days of ORD—to 1964—when it carried out a study for the President's Task Force on Manpower Conservation focusing on youth disqualified for military service.[65] The Report recommended that approximately one-third of all the young men turning 18 would, if examined, fail to qualify for induction into the Armed Forces for reasons of inadequate health or education. Most of the latter had been reared in poverty. The results of the study were used by the President to persuade Secretary of Defense McNamara to accept a large group (about 250,000 eventually) of below-standard men in the hope and expectation that through remedial assistance in the military they could be turned into effective servicemen. While the Pentagon was equivocal about the results, I reached a positive conclusion.[66]

6. A Personal Summing Up

Now that my formal assessment has been completed, the reader is free to make his own judgment about how well ORD scores on the five criteria that have been used to review its progress over the 16-year period, 1963-78. I will add my own judgment at the very end, but not before I comment briefly on some critical factors that have not been introduced up to this point but which I believe must be considered before a balanced judgment can be made. The hitherto excluded considerations deal respectively with certain developments in both the academic and political environments, each of which helps to define the parameters for any large-scale governmental research and development program in human resources and manpower.

To treat the academic issues first: most of the energy of academic economists since the university first captured the discipline has been directed to refining the intellectual corpus and perfecting successive techniques, the most recent being the dominance of mathematical model-building and econometrics. Progress in a social discipline surely depends in part on improvements in theory and advances in technique but it also depends on problem identification, data improvement, and first approximations that yield new understanding and that can contribute to policy guidance. It is my judgment that because of the pedagogic imperatives of the university which involves training and testing of students, the former always predominates to the relative neglect of the latter.

To make matters worse, the more emphasis is placed on the demonstration of technical competence by students rather than on the reliance on their written work, the greater the gap between the discipline and the inchoate world of reality.

A few points of illumination. I recall Arthur F. Burns remarking to me in the early 1960s that in his opinion his colleagues in Fayerweather Hall (the then home of the Columbia Economics Department) were off the wall since the curves which they put on the blackboard were used interchangeably to describe wages, prices, international trade, money and still other key variables.

In 1970 or 1971 the National Institute of Education asked a few consultants to discuss youth unemployment and what the schools might do to mitigate the curse. A Chicago economist, who later won the Nobel Prize, said "You know, Eli, all one has to do is wait. They'll grow out of it." I suggested that some, perhaps many, might not since they would be the victims of homicide, become drug addicts, or spend years in prison.

In 1964 Gary Becker published *Human Capital* and within a relatively few years his approach had come to dominate the field of "labor economics" at most of the country's leading universities. All that one need do is to scan the journals from the late 1960s to the present. A never-ending stream of econometric exercises has emerged in which novitiates seek to measure the influence of one or more factors on the employment and/or wages and/or career progression of individuals with differing endowments and achievements.

No one will question that Becker opened up a powerful line of analysis but the value of the inquiries informed by his approach depends in no small measure on the quality of the extant data and in most cases the data vary from poor to very poor. The combination of econometrics coming into its own and the availability of the human capital model proved a powerful combination that left its mark on ORD in the 1970s. In Glenn Cain's judgment it was all to the good,[67] but the editors of the *Industrial and Labor Relations Review* according to their recent note to prospective authors appear to have developed some second thoughts.[68]

It is an old question in new form—how much does one need to know about the institutional framework to make significant advances in understanding the operations of labor markets and the behavior of workers? I believe the answer is—a great deal.

But the world of academe has compounded the situation in still another respect. The dominance until recently of the neo-Keynesians with their reliance on a relatively small number of basic relationships to explain the level of aggregate employment must be seen as another impediment to progress. And when the theory ran afoul of an accelerating inflation after 1965, the doctrines that sought to replace Keynes, a worsening Phillips' curve, the increase in the natural rate of unemployment, and the elaboration of rational expectations created an unseemly spectacle of an analytic engine out of control. And that is where the academy stands at the beginning of 1984.

As I look back to the early days of the New Deal I find four arenas of public policy issues in the manpower orbit—unemployment, income for those who have no work or can't work, discrimination, and equality of career opportunity. This is my assessment of how well, or how poorly, we have done to cope.

With respect to unemployment the American public, as is so frequently the case, has not taken its own laws seriously and full employment is not high on the nation's agenda. I have found it irresponsible and cynical for a nation to insist that everybody, other than the sick, the injured and the elderly, take care of himself and his dependents and yet makes no serious effort to provide jobs for those who can't find an opening because there is a shortage of jobs.

We have done well in providing income for most of the elderly. Few remain in poverty once one takes in-kind transfers into account. With respect to single parents and their children even in states with relatively liberal payments, we know that money alone does not suffice. What is required, and how to intervene remain elusive. Here we need more knowledge.

Again in the case of discrimination, the record is equivocal. If one measures the progress of blacks from 1940, the gains have been appreciable; if the starting date is 1619, then progress has been abysmally slow. Many are fortunately joining the middle class; many others are regrettably still in a marginal role. Laws can help but full employment and white leadership are even more important.

With respect to expanding career opportunities for those from low income homes we have made good progress since 1958 when the Congress passed the National Defense Education Act. But the broadest opportunities are those providing for young people who are qualified to enter college. There is a group who never get properly educated in the basics without which most of them are doomed to a blighted future. We must get our public educational system to work better and it cannot do so all by itself. Improvements in the economy and in the country are also needed. Youngsters will make the effort to learn if they see some hope of benefiting. But such hope is absent for many who are brought up without a father, on welfare grants and are educated by teachers who fear or dislike them.

Some people believe that Congress has appropriated too much money in the past for these programs. My concern is different: our return per dollar expended has been relatively small and it is that issue which we must address.

Ours is a democracy and Congress' main task is to appropriate money to help achieve federal objectives, but it is forced to rely primarily on lower levels of government and the private sector to transform the dollars which it appropriates into useful goods and services. But the instrumentalities through which Congress is forced to work have their own objectives and priorities with the result that the efficiency and efficacy of federal dollar outlays are greatly reduced. To complicate matters further, the political arena contributes to an instability in administration, the dominance of an annual budgetary cycle, log-rolling in the halls of the Congress, and a calculus in which political gain is frequently at odds with program accomplishment.

We are now at the end. ORD in my view was on balance a highly successful effort. It must be adjudged that much more successful considering the sorry state of academe on which it was largely dependent for research proposals and for their implementation and on that unique American institution, the Congress, for financing, redesign and sustained support.

Appendix

From my perspective, Conservation of Human Resources (CHR), Columbia University, made significant contributions in opening up or addressing the following lines of analysis: the pluralistic economy, producer services, health manpower, comparative manpower studies (Europe and Japan), metropolitanism and suburbanization, the labor market as an information system, labor market segmentation, measuring public output, professional women, regional econometric models, and the theory of human resources.

I am listing below some of the more important research projects carried out by CHR that were supported in whole or in part by ORD during the period 1963-78.

Dale L. Hiestand. *Economic Growth and Employment Opportunities for Minorities* (New York: Columbia University Press, 1964).

Eli Ginzberg, Dale L. Hiestand, and Beatrice G. Reubens. *The Pluralistic Economy* (New York: McGraw-Hill Book Company, 1965).

James W. Kuhn. *Scientific and Managerial Manpower in Nuclear Industry* (New York: Columbia University Press, 1966).

Harry I. Greenfield. *Manpower and the Growth of Producer Services* (New York: Columbia University Press, 1966).

Harry I. Greenfield with Carol Brown. *Allied Health Manpower: Trends and Prospects* (New York: Columbia University Press, 1969).

Dean Morse. *The Peripheral Worker* (New York: Columbia University Press, 1969).

Eli Ginzberg with Miram Ostow. *Men, Money, and Medicine* (New York: Columbia University Press, 1969).

Beatrice G. Reubens. *The Hard-to-Employ: European Programs* (New York: Columbia University Press, 1970).

Thomas M. Stanback, Jr. and Richard Knight. *The Metropolitan Economy: The Process of Employment Expansion* (New York: Columbia University Press, 1970).

Ivar E. Berg. *Education and Jobs: The Great Training Robbery* (New York: Praeger Publishers, 1970).

Dale L. Hiestand. *Changing Careers After 35* (New York: Columbia University Press, 1971).

Charles Brecher. *Upgrading Blue Collar and Service Workers* (Baltimore: Johns Hopkins Press, 1972).

Ivar E. Berg (ed.). *Human Resources and Economic Welfare: Essays in Honor of Eli Ginzberg* (New York: Columbia University Press, 1972).

Stanley Friedlander with Robert Shick. *Unemployment in the Urban Core: An Analysis of 30 Cities with Policy Recommendations* (New York: Praeger Publishers, 1972).

Boris Yavitz and Dean Morse. *The Labor Market: An Information System* (New York: Praeger Publishers, 1973).

Richard Knight. *Employment Expansion and Metropolitan Trade* (New York: Praeger Publishers, 1973).

Charles Brecher. *Where Have All the Dollars Gone? Public Expenditures for Human Resources Development in New York City, 1961-1971* (New York: Praeger Publishers, 1974).

Alice M. Yohalem with Captain Quentin B. Ridgeley. *Desegregation and Career Goals: Children of Air Force Families* (New York: Praeger Publishers, 1974).

Marcia Freedman with Gretchen Maclachlan. *Labor Markets: Segments and Shelters* (Montclair: Allanheld, Osmun & Company, 1976).

Eli Ginzberg. *The Human Economy* (New York: McGraw-Hill Book Company, 1976).

Robert Cohen. *The Corporation and the City* (NTIS PB284371/AS, 1978).

David Lewin, Raymond D. Horton, and James W. Kuhn. *Manpower Utilization and Collective Bargaining in Local Government* (Montclair: Allanheld, Osmun & Company, 1979).

Alfred S. Eichner and Charles Brecher. *Controlling Social Expenditures: The Search for Output Measures* (Montclair: Allanheld, Osmun & Company, 1979).

Alice M. Yohalem. *The Careers of Professional Women: Commitment and Conflict* (Montclair: Allanheld, Osmun & Company, 1979).

Beatrice G. Reubens. *The Youth Labor Supply: A Comparative Sudy* (Montclair: Allanheld, Osmun & Company, 1979).

Matthew Drennan. *Regional Econometric Models: New York and Baltimore* (forthcoming).

A brief discussion of each of the foregoing together with related research investigations supported by other funding sources are set out in *The Fortieth Anniversary Report, 1979* of the Conservation Project.

NOTES

1. Eli Ginzberg. *The Human Economy* (New York: McGraw Hill, 1976).

2. Eli Ginzberg. *The House of Adam Smith* (New York: Columbia University Press, 1934).

3. See Abraham Pais. *Subtle is the Lord: The Science and the Life of Albert Einstein* (New York: Oxford University Press, 1982).

4. U.S. Department of Labor, Employment and Training Administration. *Research and Development: A 16-Year Compendium (1963-1978)* (Washington, DC., 1979).

5. Gordon I. Swanson and Jon Michaelson, editors. *Manpower Research and Labor Economies* (Beverly Hills: Sage Publications, 1979).

6. National Academy of Sciences, Committee on Department of Labor Manpower Research and Development. *Knowledge and Policy in Manpower,* Washington, DC, 1975.

7. Peter Barth. "Labor Market Operations: A Review of Research," in (5) above, pp. 180-81.

8. National Manpower Council. *Womanpower* (New York: Columbia University Press, 1957).

9. See *Industrial and Labor Relations Review* 17, No. 3 (April 1964).

10. *The Journal of Human Resources* 1, No. 1 (Summer 1966).

11. *Compendium,* p. 383 ff.

12. Ibid., p. 381.

13. Ibid.

14. Ibid., pp. 388-514.

15. Lawrence R. Klein. *Baker's Dozen: Abstracts of 13 Doctoral Dissertations Completed Under Manpower Administration Research Grants,* Manpower Research Monograph No. 27, 1973.

_____ , *Abstracts of Seven Doctoral Dissertations Completed Under Manpower Administration Research Grants,* Manpower Research Monograph No. 34, 1975.

_____ , *A Popularized Version of 21 Doctoral Dissertations,* R&D Monograph 70, 1979.

16. Clark Kerr. "The Intellectual Role of the Neorealists in Labor Economics," *Industrial Relations* 22, No. 2 (Spring 1983), pp. 298 ff.

17. Wassily Leontief. "Theoretical Assumptions and Nonobserved Facts." *American Economic Review* (March 1971), p. 1 ff.

18. *Compendium,* pp. 136-145.

19. June O'Neill. *Review of the National Longitudinal Surveys* (Washington, DC: The Urban Institute, 1982).

20. *Compendium,* pp. 144-145.

21. Herbert Parnes. "The National Longitudinal Surveys: An Interim Assessment." *Manpower Research and Labor Economics,* p. 227.

22. Ibid., pp. 575-576.

23. *Compendium,* p. 569.

24. Ibid., pp. 575-576.

25. Ibid., p. 10.

26. Ibid., p. 13.

27. Ibid., p. 21.

28. Ibid., pp. 66-68.

29. Ibid., p. 68.

30. Ibid., p. 69.

31. Ibid., p. 69.

32. Ibid., p. 72.

33. Ibid., Sections 1 and 2.

34. Board of Directors, Manpower Demonstration Research Corporation. *Summary and Findings of the National Supported Work Demonstration* (Cambridge: Ballinger Publishers, 1980).

35. *Compendium,* pp. 371-379.

36. Ibid., p. 5.

37. Ibid., pp. 9, 13.

38. Ibid., p. 16.

39. Ibid., p. 23.

40. Ibid., p. 73.

41. Ibid., p. 90.

42. Ibid., p. 106.

43. Ibid., pp. 78, 111.

44. Ibid., pp. 118, 121.

45. Ibid., p. 134.

46. Ibid., pp. 150-151.

47. Ibid., p. 171.

48. Ibid., pp. 170-171.

49. Michael L. Wachter. "Primary and Secondary Markets: A Critique of the Dual Approach," *Brookings Papers on Economic Activity* 3, 1974, pp. 637-680.

50. Richard B. Freeman. "Troubled Workers in the Labor Market," *Discussion Paper Number 881,* Harvard Institute of Economic Research, February 1982, p. 25.

51. *Compendium,* p. 235.

52. Ibid., p. 239.

53. Ibid., pp. 232-233.

54. Ibid., p. 232.

55. Ibid., pp. 271-272.

56. Ibid., p. 238.

57. Ibid., p. 184.

58. Ibid., p. 218.

59. Ibid., pp. 311-326.

60. Ibid., pp. 313-314.

61. Ibid., pp. 194-201.

62. Ray F. Marshall and Vernon M. Briggs, Jr. *The Negro and Apprenticeship* (Baltimore: The Johns Hopkins University Press, 1967).

63. *Compendium,* p. 213.

64. Ibid., pp. 255, 258-271.

65. Ibid., p. 17.

66. Eli Ginzberg. *The School/Work Nexus: Transition of Youth from School to Work,* Phi Delta Kappa Foundation, 1980.

67. Glenn G. Cain. "Research on Labor Supply and the Demand for Labor," *Manpower Research and Labor Economics,* pp. 133-178.

68. *Industrial and Labor Relations Review,* 36, No. 3 (April 1983), p. 480.

A Research Agenda
for Employment
and Training Policy
in the Eighties

Daniel H. Saks

Many analysts regard "policy research" as a contradiction in terms. The only kind of research that many who make or influence decisions want to see are "findings" that confirm the wisdom of their past judgments and current policy positions. A substantial fraction of research supported by policymakers is exactly of this advocacy variety. My relatively brief experience in Washington did not, however, turn me into a complete cynic on this question. I have seen situations where good research has changed people's minds and even situations where a demonstrated public interest prevailed over a private gain. That sort of research is the focus of this agenda for policy research on employment and training programs.

Good policy research should result in good programs. And good employment and training programs have as a defining characteristic the increasing of *potential earnings* of participants above what they would otherwise have been. There may be other good or bad consequences of such programs. The ones I care about are increases in lifetime potential compensation from the labor market. Even where an employment and training program is designed to redistribute income within the economy, it is redistribution that takes the form of higher subsequent earnings for the participant. That is what makes it an employment and training program rather than an income transfer program.

This essay is divided into two parts. Part one develops my priorities for the Department of Labor's vastly diminished research budget. It argues that good data collection is the primary federal research role. None of the important policy questions can be resolved without good data, and the collection of such data is the unique responsibility of the federal authorities. At current budget levels, the first responsibility is to maintain existing longitudinal data sets. Then we must begin to collect adequate data on program participants and similar nonparticipants so we can determine whether programs are working and under what conditions. Even a bare bones research effort of this type would exhaust current budgets of the Office of Research and Evaluation of the Employment and Training Administration. I argue that the level of research expenditures should be closer to the levels of the Administration's original request for 1984 and to the levels that prevailed in the late 1970s.

The second part of this essay elaborates a more complete agenda for research and is directed to researchers and funders of all sorts. It follows what I take to be the natural set of questions to ask about an employment and training system. Finding the answers to these questions is the rationale for an employment and training research policy. The questions are:

1. *Who* should be the target of employment and training programs?

2. *What* are the best potential "treatments" or sequences of "treatments" for specific types of potential participants?

3. *How* should the employment and training system be organized and financed to best deliver the appropriate services to the appropriate participants?

Even though these three questions will be treated in separate subsections, it should be noted that there is potential interplay among the three types of questions. For example, if members of a particular group are in trouble in the labor market yet no employment and training program would help them, they should not be a target for such programs. Similarly, if members of a particular group will not participate in a program, they should not be a target for participation in that program. So these three questions define interrelated components in the design of an effective employment and training system.

I. Research Priorities for the Employment and Training Administration in the Eighties

With the end of the massive research and development efforts of the Youth Office, federal support for employment and training research is now almost totally concentrated in the Office of Research and Evaluation of the Employment and Training Administration. Table 1 shows the course of budget authority and outlays for that office by itself over the past seven years:

Table 1. Budget for Office of Research and Evaluation, Employment and Training Administration (in millions of dollars)

	1978	1979	1980	1981	1982	1983	1984
Budget Authority	18.8	21.3	21.3	21.3	7.9	14.3	12.2
Outlays	15.8	18.4	19.5	14.6	19.4	11.9	13.1

Readers will note the substantial if erratic reduction in expenditures under the Reagan Administration, though had it not been for the parochial intervention of a Democratic committee chairman, budget authority in 1984 would have returned at the Administration's request to the much higher nominal level of the late 1970s. I am sorry to note that the Administration's budget requests for 1985 are only for current services. In the face of such cutbacks, what should the research priorities of the Employment and Training Administration be?

The most important research function of the federal government in this area is collecting what might be called "problem" data for analysis of why poor earnings are generated and how actual and potential programs might raise such earnings. Private individuals will not collect or disseminate such data since the costs vastly exceed any potential private benefits. It also makes little sense for states to collect data that would be useful to all of them and might make some of them seem incompetent. Valid empirical research depends first on good data and the federal government must be the unit of government to collect it.

The most important type of data for the government to collect is longitudinal information on the same individuals through time. This type of data has two unique virtues. First, it allows us to observe and control for effects of differences among people that persist through time. And this sort of population heterogeneity is one of the main problems for employment and training policy. Who should participate in such programs and how can we sort out program effects from unobserved differences among people? Longitudinal data are extremely helpful for answering such questions. Second, such data can help us identify answers to the questions that have the greatest impact on federal budget policy: how do decisions about work, family, consumption, and other matters in one period affect results in some subsequent period. The essence of employment and training investments is trading lower earnings now for higher earnings later. How these investments occur and how they might be improved are the key research questions for us. But similar questions arise for Medicaid, Medicare, AFDC, Social Security, and the disability programs.

Readers will recognize that I am arguing for the National Longitudinal Surveys (NLS) as the single most important research function of the Employment and Training Administration. That item is where I would draw the wagons in a circle; of course, I hope it would not come to that. I am saying that it is the starting point.

This means that we should not let such longitudinal panels stop for transitory budget savings. The reason is simple. The costs of reconstituting such a sample when reason finally prevails are enormous. Consider the resource costs alone. The new youth cohort of the NLS cost about $2.5 million to start up. The entire NLS with all of its cohorts will cost less than twice that to maintain. But the real cost of stopping a cohort is in having to wait for years to build up enough history on individuals to get answers to important questions. Can we really afford to wait a decade to reconstitute a panel with enough history to answer questions we need answered about who is in trouble in the labor market, why, and what the probable course of earnings of program participants might have been in the absence of program participation?

My desire to keep the NLS alive does not mean I believe it to be the most sensible way to meet federal longitudinal data responsibilities in this area for all time. Just because Labor Department personnel had the foresight to initiate the NLS, why should it continue to be a primary responsibility of the Employment and Training Administration? Other longitudinal panels have been collected by other agencies. It is time for a coordinated approach to such data and it is time for the design and acquisition of such data to be passed on to the independent data collection agencies where they belong. The resources and the responsibilities for the NLS should probably now be turned over the the Bureau of Labor Statistics where decisions about data needs and costs can be shared better both within and across agencies and where decisions about how to change the size and duration of particular cohorts could be made on statistical grounds and not on the vagaries of political interests in active labor market policies. So when I argue for not using the NLS as the bridge over a temporary budget crisis, I am not arguing for immunity—only for a jury trial by its peers and a restraining order to prevent irreparable damage.

I would, however, go much further than simply keeping NLS from dying. The major policy responsibility of the

Employment and Training Administration is to find out whether its programs are working and to identify which programs work best for which potential participants. Data are required that link subsequent labor market outcomes to specific "treatments" and sequences of "treatments" for the disadvantaged. And, of course, we need variation in "treatments" or controls in order to make some judgment about program effectiveness. The Continuous Longitudinal Manpower Survey (CLMS) was a complete failure at answering the most important policy questions about the programs. All we learned was that certain broad categories of program *appeared* to be more effective for women than men in the mid-1970s. The Labor Department's refusal to collect adequate process data must be rectified if we are to have any idea about how to improve the employment and training system and not just whether to keep it.

This need for good process and outcome data in sufficient detail to evaluate programs at least in major states is particularly acute under the current Job Training Partnership Act, since so much authority has passed to the states with so little federal monitoring of activities. In a couple of years, Congress will want to know whether the Job Training Partnership Act is nothing but a transfer of funds to the states. And the states will want to know what programs are effective for which groups in which circumstances. Process and outcomes must be better linked. The CLMS was only a poor start. The message is not to scuttle CLMS-type activities but rather to expand them and do them correctly. And next time, we should not have time and resources drained by the sort of unsatisfactory official analysis that accompanied release of each CLMS wave. If the lack of an official analysis makes some bureaucrats cringe, then it simply illumines more sharply the problem of trying to do nonadvocacy research in the current institutional setting and Congress might well consider how to make program evaluation more independent.

Program data collection should be linked to participant data and these should be linked to control group data such as the NLS or other federal longitudinal data surveys. Further, we need to collect data on the participation process itself so we can better learn how to adjust our results for selection bias (programs appearing to work or not work because the unobserved characteristics of the participants were systematically biased toward success or failure). Put simply, we need to understand how people get selected or select themselves for services. Not only is that question important in its own right, but it is essential to sorting out program impacts from selection impacts. This whole program data collection effort will cost at least as much as the NLS and would exhaust current ETA research budgets. Linkages with Social Security and other program administration data can give us more information for the dollar, but it will still be hard to collect much program evaluation data at required levels of detail and stay within current budget levels.

In order for this system to work well, other activities are required that could easily be done if we could return to the budget levels of the late seventies. First, the data need to be available in a highly subsidized, well-designed, on-line database system so that researchers with a microcomputer and a modem can easily use the data. The National Opinion Research Center and The Ohio State University are taking only the first steps toward such a system now. Second, an independent committee needs to be established by ETA to decide how to add special questions to the NLS and how to add regularly new entrants to the cohorts in the sample. The model should be the way access is arranged for the federal research facilities in the natural sciences. I reiterate this point below, but we need to close the loop in social science research between anomalous findings and the generation of new data to shed light on mysteries. And we also need new entrants to the cohorts so we can sort out vintage changes from maturation effects within cohorts.

Finally, we need to provide small grants to researchers to help with the analysis. The model should be the dissertation grants program. Even senior researchers can occasionally be hired in return for summer money, research and clerical assistance, graduate student support and access to good data. And if the senior researchers need more, they are more likely to find funding elsewhere. The highest payoff is probably from using young academic researchers.

In this section, I have outlined what I would do with the level of research budgets observed in the late 1970s. I have not included any funds for evaluation of potential new programs (so-called demonstration or pilot projects) because my conclusion from our experience in the 1970s is that such research is costly relative to what we might learn. Of course, if states can be talked into planned variations that can be evaluated, the federal government could cheaply and effectively do some of that evaluation. But the program money would have to come out of programs and the federal government would have to be able to walk away from some of those demonstrations on the grounds that the program operators made serious evaluation impossible.

What follows are some more specific proposals for research at budget levels in excess of those in place at the end of the 1970s. They represent some of my wish list for foundations and agencies of all sorts. I reiterate, however, that almost none of them are feasible or even worthwhile unless the basic data base requirements are taken care of first.

II. Who, What, and How?

Who Should Be Helped?

Since the goal of employment and training programs is to improve unsatisfactory earnings, the first task is to identify the sources of low earnings. Understanding the generation of low earnings has two extremely important uses in the design of an employment and training system: first, it helps in identifying the appropriate target groups for such programs and, second, it plays an important role in the evaluation of programs by describing the probable course of earnings in the absence of any program intervention. Thus, good targeting and good evaluation both depend upon a good understanding of what economists call earnings functions. Of course, economists have estimated literally thousands of earnings functions over the past few decades. I would argue, however, that some new emphases are required.

Earnings functions have several components to them. First, the earnings themselves can be divided into hours of work and wages per hour. Programs may affect these components differently for different groups. Second, there are the characteristics of the earners associated with especially low earnings. These include the education, training, and work experience of the earner—all of which might be directly changed by an effective employment and training program. Other personal characteristics include the race, sex, and ethnic background of the earner. These might be associated with discrimination in the labor market and might suggest where compensatory and antidiscrimination policies could be helpful. Nonpersonal characteristics often associated with poor earnings include the industry and occupation of regular employment and the condition of the labor market in which the earner normally resides.

The third component of earnings functions includes the fixed but typically unmeasured characteristics of earners. Even though these characteristics are unmeasured, we know about them from the simple fact that earnings of apparently similar individuals differ in persistent ways. The final component of the earnings function is what might be called the shock or dislocation factor. People have good or bad years and sheer luck can propel them to a temporary or permanent change in their earnings. Even though these are random events, we can still learn about the typical size of such shocks and about the typical trajectory of earnings differentials associated with such shocks.

Economists have learned a great deal about the shape of earnings functions in the past decade.[1] We know that training programs have a greater effect on the hours of work of participants than they do on the wages of successful participants. We know that education and experience account for something like a quarter of the variance in earnings. We know that other personal variables account for perhaps a fifth of the variance of earnings. And we know that other unmeasured fixed characteristics of earners account for perhaps another quarter of the variance of earnings. We also know that almost two-thirds of any shock to normal earnings fades away within one year. In short, we can label perhaps half the correlates of variance in earnings observed in the population. Whether one considers the glass to be half full or half empty is not entirely a matter of taste. Understanding the unobserved portions of the earnings function needs to become a high priority if we are to understand how to match programs to individuals. Progress requires cooperative research projects among social science disciplines.

I would identify the following important research issues on earnings functions for consideration:

1. Why should hours of work be more responsive to employment and training programs than the wages per hour? Do employers establish a set of minimum characteristics for potential employees at a given wage and only hire those who have those characteristics? Are there differences between employment and training interventions that affect hours and interventions that affect earnings? Are some types of potential participants more susceptible to hourly earnings gains and others to hours gains?

2. How can we develop less superficial measures of personal characteristics and of personal capacities? How, for instance, do we adjust years of schooling and types of experience on the job to reflect differences in quality of those experiences that might be systematic across certain members of the population? One particularly acute problem in the employment and training area is that we are interested in programs that affect long term earnings and yet we want to evaluate programs quickly. This means that we have to develop tests that can measure changes in earnings-related characteristics of individuals. These should help define the content of programs as well. There already exist several tests for certain types of vocational skills and these need to be developed further. Since the Army is currently engaged in fairly elaborate analysis of skills required for certain jobs, more collaboration between civilian and military employment and training interests might pay off. The crucial point is to develop measures of skills and other characteristics which are in turn related to subsequent earnings gains. Indeed, such tests would be validated by earnings gains.

3. We need to learn more about the nature of those fixed, unmeasured characteristics that account for at least a quarter of the variance in earnings in the population and are, I would

argue, the most crucial portion in understanding concentrated earnings problems. Econometric techniques can identify for study individuals with persistently low earnings given their other characteristics. The defect of current social science research is the alienation of analysis from data collection. Unlike the natural sciences where a peculiar finding results in the design of new tests and the acquisition of new data, in the social sciences that linkage is much less evident. Those individuals with large negative fixed characteristics need to receive in-depth analyses. Simple massaging of existing data sets is not going to resolve these questions about health, motivation, decisionmaking and other factors. Even Herbert Parnes, who has collected one of the most important data sets available to modern social scientists has noted this problem:

> After examining a computer print-out of the relevant information for an individual, one generally longs for an opportunity to talk to her or him for an account of why things happened as they did and how this respondent reacted.[2]

The loop must be closed to understand why some are special and what this implies about employment and training programs for them. This might involve both special interviews and also planned variation in providing employment and training strategies for such people. One way of identifying a problem is to see what helps remove it.

4. It is important to explore differences in the recovery of individuals from negative earnings shocks or dislocations. These are typically modeled as first order Markov processes; is this the best characterization? How do the fade-out rates (transition probabilities) vary with the characteristics of the individuals involved and their situations? Neither industry nor occupation are good predictors of how rapidly an earnings shock fades away, but general levels of unemployment in the local labor market are important. Why? One of the

difficulties facing programs for dislocated workers (workers with decent jobs who suddenly find themselves unemployed because of technological advance, competition, or reduced demand for their products) is determining who will likely be in long term trouble and who will recovery quickly. This was a special problem of the Trade Adjustment Assistance Act programs. It is a particular worry because provision of attractive programs for those who rebound quickly by themselves might delay their recovery and waste scarce resources. Learning how to target such programs means learning which individuals will have the slow fade-out rate for shocks. Again, it may mean in-depth analyses after they are identified.

5. How do low earners move among labor markets, firms, jobs within firms, and occupations? We have little understanding of the way in which unobserved characteristics affect both low earnings and mobility decisions. It may be that one of the better employment and training strategies for many involves incentives to workers and employers for mobility. What we seem to know from the literature on mobility is that there are movers and there are stayers. Why? Are these fixed, immutable characteristics? Can we find some way of distinguishing between these two categories before the fact as an aid in targeting various programs. Again, it requires statistical analysis to identify the stayers and clever probing to figure out why.

What Should Be Done? Toward Better Program Design for Particular Groups

If we have learned anything over the past two decades about employment and training programs, it is that different programs work better for different groups (and that some do not work at all). Discussion of research on program effectiveness should therefore be organized by particular groups among those most likely to be distressed workers. This is not the place for a detailed argument about who is likely to be a distressed worker in the 1980s since I have only recently reviewed the evidence about that.[3] I will simply discuss program research issues for the four key groups that might be in labor market distress: 1) youth having difficulty breaking into the labor market; 2) disadvantaged adults with low normal earnings; 3) dislocated experienced workers; and 4) distressed older workers.

Before turning to programs for those particular groups, I will consider macroeconomic policy because that affects all these groups. There is a division of labor in economic policy for dealing with the problems of distressed workers. There are the cyclically unemployed and underemployed and for them, *by definition,* the best program is a buoyant labor market. The other distressed workers are those who are, again by definition, structurally underemployed, unemployed, or poverty wage workers. The demarcation between these sets has been the subject of debates among economists for generations.[4] The more recent form of the argument is over whether there is a level of overall unemployment below which the inflation rate begins to accelerate. Whether or not such a point exists, most agree that there are limits to how much overall macroeconomic stimulus can accomplish in eliminating unemployment and poverty level earnings. Because the limits on general demand stimulus are so important to employment and training policy, an agenda for research on macroeconomic issues belongs in the list of research issues discussed here. My entries are:

1. How should business cycle conditions affect the mix of services provided by the employment and training system? This is a broad question on which many have already taken a position. For example, I have argued[5] that the current employment and training system with no public service employment and few support services might have made sense

in the more normal labor market of the late 1970s and the programs of that period might have made more sense now in dealing with the long term unemployed who have exhausted their unemployment benefits and for whom welfare is not a viable option. Part of my argument rests on the difficulty of enforcing a work test for the long term unemployed who might otherwise be helped by extended unemployment insurance benefits during such a severe recession. Offering help in the form of a job may assure fewer adverse incentives. But this is only a hypothesis worth examining. Are long term unemployed better off with a public job and is society better off transferring aid to them via such a mechanism? The supported work experiments examined the effectiveness of the well-designed sheltered workshop for the disadvantaged, but we have not adequately explored its value for the cyclically unemployed. Please note, I am not naive enough to think this would be a research priority of the current Administration. But it is a strategy that ought to be of interest, especially in the context of workfare proposals. The parallel question is whether it makes sense to spend much money on training when unemployment is this high? Will such workers at best simply displace other workers? The displacement question is just as important for training programs as it was for public service employment programs.

2. What sets the limits for the employment-expanding possibilities of overall economic policy and how do these limits vary? Demographic characteristics have been emphasized in past research, but to say that there are more youngsters and women in the labor force and that the unemployment rate is higher is simply to relabel our ignorance. We know that unemployment consists of short spells by many and long spells by a few. We must disentangle those two components in our analysis of the relation between labor market conditions and inflation. Short spells might actually increase as the labor market becomes tighter and there is more job mobility; but why is long term unemployment so

relatively unresponsive? What structural programs would increase the responsiveness of the long term unemployed to buoyant labor markets? An additional limit on use of macropolicy to reduce labor market distress has been the inflationary impact of capacity utilization on product markets. As recently as 1973, labor and product markets appeared to tighten simultaneously. In the late 1970s, it appeared that produce market pressures on prices occurred well before labor market pressures. Why should such a disconnection occur?

3. How might government reduce inflationary labor market pressures without incurring such excessive costs among those who are at the margin of distress or poverty? We have known for some time that it takes an extra 1 percent unemployed for two years to lower the inflation rate by 1 percentage point. That relationship has held for some years and it gives an idea of how costly it is to fight inflation through the labor market, especially when poor workers suffer disproportionately from increases in unemployment. Are there ways of targeting deflationary pressures to increase their efficiency or are there ways of arranging real wage cuts in response to shocks like the OPEC oil price increases without incurring such heavy social costs? In our decentralized labor markets, the idea of income policies to coordinate such reductions is attractive and may yet be needed in the 1980s. Understanding how wage increases diffuse through the economy thus becomes important for understanding how to coordinate anti-inflation and employment and training strategies.

We turn now to a discussion of program research for each of the four distressed groups enumerated above. It should be noted that the Labor Department has supported so much research over the past two decades that many of the issues mentioned below have been touched upon in one project or another and so what follows is an agenda for continuing research as well as new research.[6]

Distressed Youth

Although youth unemployment rates are high, most youth have relatively little trouble entering the labor market. However, a concentrated group of youth (somewhere between 5 and 10 percent) do have considerable difficulty. They suffer long term unemployment and this results in lower earnings later in their lives. Youth from poor families with poor education and, if black, the additional problems of discrimination face horrendous problems in the labor market. An enormous amount of extremely useful research was mounted in the 1970s. I would recommend the following topics for further consideration:

1. How should alternative schools be designed for high school dropouts and potential dropouts? The Youth Incentive Entitlement Pilot Projects showed that the offer of a job and an alternative school had little impact on dropping out of school, but it did cause many who had already dropped out to go into an alternative school program. There is much less indication of any impact on graduation rates, though perhaps some earnings impacts. In the new Administration's unseemly haste to close down the previous Administration's research efforts, many important questions were left unanswered. Was it the offer of a job or the offer of an alternative school or both that caused this return to a schooling program? What was the impact of that alternative schooling on the functional literacy of those who participated? These key questions should be the subject of a major research effort on youth. The objective should be to incorporate the elements of alternative schools as regular institutional features of the high school programs. There is, to be sure, a great danger in rigid design of special programs for potential high school dropouts. This restriction on student mobility, however, is likely to be more than outweighed by the dreadful consequences of simply ignoring such groups. Everyone is now talking about the design of excellent high schools, by which they mean better high schools for the better students. I

am talking here about excellent programs in the high schools for the lower tail of the achievement distribution.

2. What do the noncollege bound students need to learn in high school? There is often a presumption that simple vocational skills are the best subjects for such students. There seems to be ample evidence that the secondary vocational education system, while more costly than other forms of high school, does not generally provide long term earnings gains for its graduates. Clerical and industrial education programs do provide some short term earnings gains. What are the sets of vocational skills taught most usefully in a classroom setting and are there ways of increasing the effectiveness of such instruction? Can we identify general vocational skills that should be taught? Should we not also be teaching young people reasoning and problemsolving skills? Cognitive psychologists have been making considerable strides in understanding how to teach such skills to young people with relatively low IQs. Should such reasoning and functional literacy skills be taught more and should out-of-school youth also get such training? How can we encourage mixtures of formal classroom training with on-the-job training such as are found in the "dual system" of West Germany. While that system cannot easily be translated to the United States because of substantially different traditions and institutions, the cooperative education movement is, perhaps, a viable model on which to build better educational experiences for noncollege bound youth.

3. What do employers really want in their entry level workers? It is my impression that upper level officers of large companies say they want workers who are *generally* trained and can therefore learn the specific skills required at a firm. Lower-level supervisors, on the other hand, are reputed to want workers who already know the specific skills that are required. It would be useful to analyze what kinds of skills are required and where those skills are best taught. We cannot simply rely on the market to handle this problem

because the schools have generally done a poor job of trying to serve the poor students. Irrelevant instruction may explain why dropping out is so common for some groups and places.

4. Job Corps needs to be continually monitored. It is the most successful and unique of the American employment and training programs for the severely disadvantaged and, because its cost will always seem excessive to some, it is necessary continually to be able to make the case that the rate of return is high. It is also important to discover if that rate of return should start to fall. We should also explore how elements of the Job Corps program might be used in less expensive programs of a nonresidential character. In my view, Job Corps should be the centerpiece of the employment and training system and it should be recognized as a laboratory for design elements throughout the system.

Disadvantaged Adults

It has been the hope, particularly after the retargeting of programs in the early 1960s, that employment and training programs could raise the earnings of those workers whose normal earnings were below subsistance. It was an alternative to welfare. We now know from the negative income tax experiments that creating work incentives under welfare will be expensive because of the necessary adverse work incentives for those formerly above the break-even level. That means there is even more value to raising potential earnings of the poor through effective employment and training programs. Here are my candidates for research:

1. How can income transfer programs be better linked to employment and training programs? It is clear that a simple unified negative income tax is not desirable unless it is linked with the adoption of a simple flat-rate tax—and I do not consider that very feasible. Different groups should be subject to different tax rates and income guarantees depending on their family situation, employment prospects, etc. Employment and training programs can have a place in such

a design. For one thing, such programs can help select out those who do not need labor market help. That has not been a popular perspective in this country, though it appears to be implicit in the programs of Sweden and some other countries. I again mention the possibilities of sorting the long term unemployed according to labor market attachment by offering benefits (such as training or job subsidies) that can ony be used in the labor market.

2. Why are job subsidies so ineffective despite the fact that economists find them so desirable? We have learned that employers do not respond much to employment incentives; there are reasons one can imagine, including red tape, worry about tax audits, certification by the government that those receiving vouchers are "turkeys," etc. But we do not know the answer, nor do we know if there are effective ways of offsetting these defects. Job subsidies to be used in the public or private sector ought to be the best way of doing targeted job creation. We know it is not. Why? Can some experiments be devised to find out? While the Employment Opportunity Pilot Project was poorly designed, the question it was supposed to answer still remains.

3. Why did CETA and other programs seem to work better for women than for men? Is it that the women were of higher quality because of sex descrimination in the labor market or other reasons? Is their access to comparable opportunities less? What does the answer imply about improving the design of programs for women and for men? Are there any useful interventions for adult men?

4. What is the relationship between low normal earnings and physical and psychological health and what does the linkage imply about the design of programs? A recent paper by some Vanderbilt colleagues suggests that those with fewer than eight years of formal education are three times as likely as high school graduates to have common diseases including cardiovascular, pulmonary, and musculoskeletal.[7] This

would be one important mechanism linking low earnings between periods in an individual's life. Low education is correlated with low earnings. Is it a cause or effect of poor health? Answering such questions requires new types of interdisciplinary research and an alliance between social and biological sciences that has not been the norm in the past.

5. Is there addictive behavior being generated by human resource programs as some conservatives suggest? Does government help breed dependency and are there some types of help that are more likely to breed the sort of independence that most of us want program participants to achieve? The question has not been taken seriously, but I believe it should be. In more formal terms, it is a question about how far back in the evolution of a person's career state dependency (in the Markovian sense) persists. Sociologists have pioneered methods for analyzing such problems using long panels of data and it is an important and tractable issue. How big is the effect and how can it be minimized?

6. Why is the serious bifurcation in the labor market for blacks occurring and what, if anything, can employment and training programs do about it? While earnings of young educated blacks has been rising to parity with similar young white cohorts, the relative earnings and income of less educated blacks has been falling so that average income differentials between the races have stayed remarkably constant. Many less educated blacks are simply dropping out of our statistics. Why? What are they doing? Are things getting worse or do they have better alternatives? Has the type of discrimination faced by blacks in the labor market become quality discrimination (blacks have to be better than whites to get similar jobs) or have education and training opportunities been getting worse for blacks at the low end of the distribution? Are new programs required and could some planned variation or experiments be devised to identify better programs? A major effort needs to be undertaken to find the equivalent of Job Corps for such disadvantaged adults.

Perhaps an intelligent program of prevention should be put in place and those who are too old should simply receive income transfers. That decision should not be made on the basis of current knowledge.

Dislocated Workers

Experienced workers with good jobs have been laid off in record numbers over the past four years and this has led to a revival of the automation scare of the 1960s. I would hardly deny that the economy has been undergoing change and that we are moving closer to the day when no larger a share of the workforce will be involved in manufacturing than is now involved in agriculture. However, I see no reason to panic about the pace of change. Some readers may respond, "Of course he sees no reason to panic, he is a tenured professor!" This is not the place for detailed argument, but many recent problems have been associated with the recession and many will be eliminated by the recovery. It is simply too early to tell whether, for example, the upper Midwest is in a serious long term decline or whether it is suffering from the fact that we have been using high interest rates to fight the inflation for the past four years. The upper Midwest specializes in the manufacture of interest-sensitive consumer durables. What seems pretty clear from the research of the past decades is that neither industry nor occupation is a good target for programs designed to help dislocated workers. The dislocation problems are most acute when individuals are not flexibly trained and when an entire labor market deteriorates. For dislocated workers, the following research topics should be considered:

1. Can the impact of the computer be predicted from analysis of the margins of change in the current economy? There is a tendency to focus on the job-displacing consequences of the computer, but of course many jobs will be created as well. Furthermore, the effects will be indirect. Predicting the consequences of the invention and adoption of the automobile by simply focusing on what happened to

horses and carriages now seems ridiculous to us. The automobile changed our entire economy and society. So the computer will allow the development of custom production where scale economies become less and less important. This means more people will be engaged in the design and matching of products to uses. What does all this imply about the retraining of workers and about the education of new entrants into the labor force? What general skills should high schools teach for labor market careers in excess of 50 years in such a new environment?

2. Under what circumstances are retraining programs effective for dislocated workers? Are retraining programs better for women than men because they have more restricted mobility in our society and retraining might compensate for immobility? How does mobility relate to the design of retraining? The early results from the Down River demonstrations indicate poor results for retraining programs, though experimental evidence would be more persuasive on the matter. What other programs need to be linked together for long term dislocated workers? For example, are there regional development efforts that can be facilitated by retraining, or is that a strategy for which troubled regions have no comparative advantage over growing regions like the Sun Belt?

3. Can incentives be designed and tested experimentally so that firms considering plant closings can help their employees find other jobs more quickly? Either tax advantages or the employment of plant managers as consultants in the placement process might be worth trying. Could incentives for early warning of at-risk workers be provided? There is now a high level of strategy involved in the negotiations with workers in such circumstances and the game may well be a prisoner's dilemma where some social intervention would make both parties better off.

4. Can labor market adjustment be aided by facilitating the flow of information on vacancies and job seekers? The

real estate industry has managed to keep the matching of buyers and sellers private while collectively sharing information through multiple listings. Could something along those lines be developed for the labor market? Anyone who has observed the job-matching by computer available in Sweden cannot fail to be impressed. Of course, Sweden is smaller and the public job service controls the market, but it is also true that they got the idea from experiments in Texas. This might be a service that could become self-financing after awhile.

5. For those workers who become long term unemployed, are there ways of giving assistance that will speed the labor market adjustment process? Experiments with alternative employment and training vouchers for training, job subsidies, relocation assistance, and other devices might identify mechanisms with fewer long term disincentives than those found under our typical readjustment assistance programs developed in the 1970s.

Older Workers in Distress

As workers age, they become increasingly attached to particular firms and dislocation results in longer duration unemployment. For many, health and related problems suggest that the best solution is retirement. But with increasing life expectancy, employment and training programs could have a 15 year pay-back period for a 55 year old worker. With an aging population and a need to raise the retirement age, this population will become an increasing focus of employment and training efforts. Society will increasingly face decisions about who should and who should not have to work. My candidates for research include:

1. What are the impediments to part-time employment for older workers and can something be done to reduce them? Fixed fringe benefits can make part-time employees quite unattractive. Can ways be found for the government to take over some of these and for employees to share more of the

costs and benefits of such schemes? Would that reduce transfer costs by increasing labor supply?

2. Will age discrimination statutes that are easiest to enforce on firings cause the locus of any age discrimination to shift to hiring? Is it generally becoming harder to get rid of bad employees and does that work to the detriment of hiring older workers? The answers to this might require some detailed analysis of employer behavior under different rules of seniority.

3. Can planned variation or experiments be devised to figure out the most effective employment and training interventions for older workers? Should special programs be designed for them or can such people be well-served in existing programs as some recent evidence suggests?

How Should the System be Organized?

It should be no surprise, but research seems to have had less impact on the design of the delivery system than on any other component of employment and training policy. Research on delivery system issues is the most potentially threatening activity from the viewpoint of the policymaker. Yet research might inform the ideological debates and there are some topics that I would consider prime candidates for research.

I cannot resist one remark about delivery systems and our experience over the past two decades. Since the early 1970s, the system has moved increasingly to a decentralized design with states receiving increasing authority. Only one part of the system was exempted from the perpetual commotion associated with reform of the system and that was Job Corps. It is federally operated by subcontractors who are held to standards that are generally well-regarded. And it is this part of the system that has had the most consistent success with the most difficult population: severely disadvantaged youth. Someone less familiar with the politics of employment and training programs might ask why Job Corps is not the model of an effective delivery system for helping distressed workers.

There are four research questions I would suggest:

1. What is the best mix of formal statistical evaluation techniques and of institutional control mechanisms to assure an effective system? A promising research strategy would involve collaboration of political scientists and economists on comparative studies across countries. Sweden and Germany are generally reputed to have high quality systems. They subject themselves to little formal evaluation and so there is little evidence on their systems' effectiveness. On the other hand, they have created institutional arrangements and government mechanisms that reinforce standards and relevance of training and they have established a highly professional system. We have generally failed to do that, though there are some examples of outstanding programs in particular places in the U.S. Both formal evaluation *and* good institutions are essential. We need research on how to design those institutions for the particular local environments in the U.S.

2. It is now understood that in the absence of controlled experiments, it is only by modeling the selection of program participants and the goals of program operators that we can identify the impact of programs. From my point of view, formalizing the selection would help in evaluation. In fact, if selection were done by an examination (and the ironic result is that the worse the test, the easier it is to be confident of the estimates of treatment effects) then we could improve evaluation of alternative programs. If we cannot do random assignments, then we ought to consider selection tests. But we also need to understand selection issues because they are important in their own right. The government is interested in these programs in order to offset market failure and to provide new employment opportunities to workers whom employers have not especially wanted. Employers, on the

other hand, want the best workers they can find. As we have shifted the balance of the system toward business control, the likelihood of creaming will increase. That may make the programs look better to the unsophisticated, but it will make the system less effective as a remedial device. That means that research on selection becomes one of the key points of inquiry about how the new JTPA system is working.

3. One of the ideological solutions to program deficiencies under the current administration is to convert competitive or monitored programs into general block grants to states. To my way of thinking, that will generate less efficiency. The competitive pressures and the oversight will be removed. Others argue, however, that local responsibility will more than offset such effects. This is a researchable question for the sort of methodology pioneered by Richard Nathan and it should be explored further.

4. Finally, we need to explore better linkages of finance and delivery, especially in conducting industrial policy. If we have to target aid to particular industries, I would argue that we should tax those same industries in the long run to pay for the benefits. Once that is done, I frankly do not care what the aid consists of. The rise and fall of the British Industrial Training Boards can provide a good deal of insight on this approach. The point is that we need to figure out how to link the financing of employment and training and other programs with the benefits and the costs. User fees might improve programs as well as relieve tight budgets. I have argued that user fees could be a great source of improvement for the Job Service and the principle ought to apply elsewhere.

Conclusion

While research budgets for employment and training, like the programs themselves, have been reduced substantially, there are certainly many issues that could profitably be studied. The first priority of the Labor Department ought to be data collection. In a more decentralized system, the acquisition of data on outcomes, processes, and selection becomes essential if we are to know if the system is any good and if we are to improve the system.

Beyond that, I have listed a variety of research topics requiring closing the research loop to help in finding new answers rather than just in recertifying old problems. There is simply too much specialization in our research. Rigorous research across several activities and disciplines could have large payoff. But that requires coordination and leadership.

NOTES

1. See for example Lee A. Lillard and Robert J. Willis, "Dynamic Aspects of Earning Mobility," *Econometrica* 46, no. 5 (1978) pp. 985-1012; and Richard B. Freeman, "Appendix A, Troubled Workers in the Labor Market," *Seventh Annual Report, the Federal Interest in Employment and Training,* The National Commission for Employment Policy (October 1981) pp. 103-174.

2. Herbert S. Parnes, *Unemployment Experience of Individuals Over a Decade: Variations by Sex, Race and Age* (Kalamazoo, MI: W. E. Upjohn Institute for Employment Research, 1982) p. 47.

3. *Distressed Workers in the Eighties* (Washington, DC: National Planning Association, 1983) p. 70.

4. For a further discussion of the cyclical aspects of employment and training policy and the various issues raised by current policy, see my chapter on "Jobs and Training" in *Setting National Priorities: The 1984 Budget,* Joseph A. Pechman, editor (Washington, DC: The Brookings Institution, 1983) pp. 145-172.

5. Ibid.

6. Those who want to get an idea of the range of past research should see the report of the Committee on Department of Labor Manpower Research and Development, Assembly of Behavioral and Social Sciences, National Research Council, *Knowledge and Policy in Manpower: A Study of the Manpower Research and Development Program in the Department of Labor* (Washington, DC: National Academy of Sciences, 1975) p. 171.

7. Theodore Pincus and Richard Burkhauser, "Most Common Diseases Occur More Frequently in Individuals with Fewer Years of Formal Education," Vanderbilt University, 1983, mimeo.

An Administrator's Reflections

Howard Rosen

Few former federal career employees are even invited to come out of the closet of bureaucratic anonymity to reflect on programs they have administered. I immodestly accepted this invitation to discuss what I experienced and learned as the Director of the Office of Research and Development in the Department of Labor's Employment and Training Administration between 1962 and 1980 because I believe that my observations might be of interest not only to labor economists but also to students of public administration.

Let me begin by making some general comments about important differences controlling administration in the public and private sectors. Public administrators are controlled by a law, many laws or regulations. Legalism in general, and laws in particular, tend to circumscribe and influence the operation of publicly administered programs more so than in the private sector. Administrators of private programs are told by law what they cannot do. The law tells the administrators of public programs what they can do. This is a subtle but important difference affecting decisions and freedom to act.

A second important difference is the goldfish bowl environment of life in Washington. In addition to perpetual scrutiny, public administrators are held to far higher ethical and moral standards than those found in the private sector. On top of these restraints, career public administrators must maintain a neutrality and professionalism not often required in private industry.

In spite of the laws, regulations and ethical standards, public administrators are expected to be effective and perform assignments. It is my belief that administrators of government programs must be more creative, imaginative and resourceful than their counterparts in private industry if they are to achieve program objectives.

The Department of Labor's Employment and Training Administration (ETA) program was conducted during 18 years of turmoil, change and national unrest. During the 1962-80 period the country was involved in two military wars and one massive social and economic war against poverty. The Research and Development program was conducted through recessions, inflation, race riots, and active civil rights movement leading to growth in minority power and oil price shocks.

The economy changed and required new and different skills from our workforce. The share of manufacturing jobs declined from about 30 to 20 percent of total employment. Service industry employment rose from 14 to 20 percent of all jobs and the proportion of employees working for state and local governments increased from 12 to 15 percent of total employment. Despite the unprecedented entry of increasing numbers of young workers into the labor force and a 50 percent increase in our workforce, the country suffered no massive unemployment.

A social revolution was also changing the labor force participation of women. While the participation rate for men declined in every age group between the ages of 20 to 64, the rates for women increased in every age cohort. Child rearing no longer forced most women out of the labor force. Between 1962 and 1980, the labor force participation rate for women with children under the age of six more than doubled and the number of families headed by women also rose from 4.5 to 9.0 million.

The ETA social science research program was established under Title I of the Manpower Development and Training Act (MDTA) of 1962, continued under the Comprehensive Employment and Training Act (CETA) of 1973, and extended under the Job Training Partnership Act (JTPA) of 1982. The Manpower Act was passed primarily in order to offset the displacement effects of automation and technological changes in workers. During the 1960 presidential campaign, Senator Kennedy was exposed to the large number of unemployed West Virginia coal miners who had lost their jobs because of the shifts to diesel locomotives and the greater use of oil and other sources of energy than coal. He promised the people of West Virginia that, if elected president, he would try to assist them. He carried out his promise with manpower legislation which proposed to train and retrain workers who were unemployed because of automation and technological changes.

Those of us who participated in writing some sections of what eventually became the Manpower Act experienced the wondrous and mysterious ways of how legislation is prepared. At first, there was a period of intense and furious work. Our respective contributions were then collected and we never saw what the legislation looked like until it surfaced as the proposed Manpower Act. We never heard about, nor were we a party to, the negotiations as the proposed legislation drifted through the various agencies which were to participate in its implementation. Once the bill appeared on the Hill we were reactivated again to write speeches for cabinet officers and legislators during the hearings and congressional debates.

Before and after the Manpower Act was passed there was considerable contact with Swedish government officials who described their "active manpower policy" to U.S. policymakers. Under this philosophy, the Swedish government was no longer a neutral observer of developments affecting its workforce. Unemployment, industrial shifts and labor market operations were now a concern of the government. Some, but not all, of the Swedish thinking was adopted by those involved in the development of a U.S. manpower policy during the early 1960s.

Title I of the Manpower Act called for a research program that differed quite radically from those then being conducted by the Bureau of Labor Statistics (BLS) and other components of the Department of Labor. For decades, BLS had collected information contributing to our fund of knowledge about the employment and unemployment of American workers. It also collected data on wages, prices and productivity. The Bureau was not expected to be concerned with policy-oriented research. Under the Manpower Act, the Department was now directed to collect information that could shape policy and programs. We were also given the opportunity to develop and test, in operational situations, ways in which manpower programs might more effectively meet significant manpower problems.

The new legislation called for a research program that contributed to policies that would result in solutions of the problems created by ". . . changes in the structure of production and demand in the use of the Nation's human resources."[1] The research office, which was created under Title I of MDTA, was allocated $2.8 million per year between 1962 and 1970 to study, in addition to automation, the practices of employers and unions which impede the mobility of workers, appraise the adequacy of the nation's manpower development efforts and recommend programs for untrained and inexperienced youth. Armed with the imprecise and ambiguous language of the Manpower Act, we marched off to war to do away with unemployment and its causes.

Once the law was passed we discovered that it is far easier to write legislation than it is to translate legislative language into programs. An apprehensive group of federal employees met in Seymour Wolfbein's office on March 16, 1962, the day after President Kennedy signed the law.[2] To counter the perennial criticism of the underworked government employee, it should be documented that we worked an average of 10 to 12 hours a day for 7 days a week for a full year in order to launch the training and retraining programs. Substantive work was conducted on Saturdays and Sundays when the telephone switchboard was closed. The initial plans for a research program were developed in between hundreds of telephone calls and numerous speeches given around the country. The first year was a true test of our physical stamina and emotional stability.

In order to put a publicly administered research program in proper context, it may be helpful to discuss both the internal and external environment which influenced and affected some of our decisions and programs.

Internal Environment

Much has been written about the relationship between political appointees and career government employees. Each president can bring in to his administration 2,500 new appointees. The job qualifications of these policymakers and knowledge of the programs they administer may vary considerably. There is always an uncomfortable period of testing that goes on between political appointees and career employees until mutual respect and trust is developed. The research office seems to have survived a succession of policymakers by demonstrating its ability to contribute its knowledge to the needs of a variety of policymakers.

The management staff of ETA, consisting of career federal employees, was a problem of another sort. The budget responsibilities and oversight authority of the procurement process of the management personnel enabled them to exert considerable power over our activities. We had frequent disputes with the management people because of their lack of understanding of social science research and their distrust of social scientists. Most of the previous experience of the management staff had been limited to the purchase of desks, chairs and other supplies and equipment. We sought a flexibility in our work with social researchers that was foreign to their way of thinking. Until we demonstrated our usefulness to the political appointees and the operating managers of ETA's programs, our research budget was considered fair game for purposes other than research by the management personnel

Another group which contributed to a hostile environment for a research program in a mission-oriented agency was the administrators of programs such as Unemployment Insurance, the Bureau of Apprenticeship and Training (BAT) and the operators of training and retraining activities.

Our challenge was to persuade some of these administrators that a research program could be useful to them. We needed their cooperation because their programs were relevant to our mission. Furthermore, if they participated in decisions on research projects they might be more inclined to utilize our findings in their programs.

We finally worked out a strategy that proved most effective. After our annual budget increased from $2.8 to $13.0 million in 1970, we set aside a fixed sum of money that was to be used for research and development purposes for each operating component of the Employment and Training Administration. We used committees, consisting of representatives of the research office and operating agencies, to review and make decisions about research projects relevant to their missions. We learned that money is an effective tool for winning friends in the public sector of the economy.

Some examples of committee-sponsored research included an assessment of the counseling service of the Employment Service and a study of how the productivity of local employment offices could be improved. The committee also sponsored an examination of the *Dictionary of Occupational Titles* to determine its usefulness and its users. Although money was effective in reducing some of the hostility to research, we had recurrent problems in trying to persuade our peers that we were not about to invade their jurisdictions.

The Bureau of Labor Statistics was another organization that had to be assured that we were not taking over their functions. Again, money and strategy helped to ease tensions. As indicated earlier, the Manpower Act directed us to appraise the adequacy of the nation's manpower development efforts to meet foreseeable needs for workers. We asked the Bureau of Labor Statistics to conduct a pioneering survey of how American workers acquired training for their jobs.[3] This study both eased our relations with BLS and gave the country its first view of the extent of job training in the U.S.

Our one major conflict with BLS took place over their reluctance to reassess their data collection system in urban centers. We had supported the work of anthropologists who lived in ghetto areas. They reported that many minority workers had become discouraged and dropped out of the labor market. In their view, BLS surveys did not correctly measure the extent of unemployment in ghetto areas. Eventually, BLS was persuaded to examine the problem of undercounting which led to a new data series on unemployment in central cities.

The final point about our internal environment concerns our experience with the Bureau of Apprenticeship and Training. In reviewing our mandate to collect information about the training of American workers, it became obvious that although the apprenticeship system trained a relatively small number of craftsmen, it played a significant role in preparing some of the country's most skilled workers. The close relations of the personnel of BAT with the unions made it difficult to conduct any research that might appear in any way to loosen the trade unions' control of a training system that affected the supply of workers.

In order to learn more about the apprenticeship system and to conduct studies to modernize it we devised a strategy that would avoid a confrontation with either BAT personnel or the unions. Our plan called for the development of a model apprenticeship program that could be used as a comparison by unions and employers now conducting programs. We proposed a new system for realistically determining the number of hours required for learning the plumber and pipefitter trade.

We asked Dr. John Dunlop of Harvard, who was trusted and respected by union leaders, to review our plan and, if it proved acceptable to him, to use his negotiating skills to persuade the unions to go along with our proposed study. After he approved our approach, he encouraged trade union leaders to participate in the preparation of a model apprenticeship program which was developed at Purdue University. The results of the study were published in a series of monographs which were widely distributed and contributed to the modernization of some apprenticeship programs.

To sum up our internal environment problems, we succeeded in having research and development accepted in a mission-oriented agency only after we demonstrated the usefulness of our findings. Research could be conducted if we avoided face-to-face confrontations and developed strategies that would not directly challenge programs or jurisdictions. Money was helpful, but the committee system which involved the potential users of research was also effective in developing cooperative working relationships. Finally, knowledge of institutional politics and access to persons who could help us to achieve our objectives proved to be of inestimable value.

The External Environment

The most important component of our external environment was the research community. We were launching a program that required researchers who were interested in problems of unemployment, underemployment, labor market operations, discrimination, skill training and the special difficulties faced by the "economically disadvantaged" of our society. In surveying the literature of the early and mid-1960s, we were struck by the small number of scholars who were studying the problems specified by MDTA and its amendments. Most of the social scientists whose backgrounds and experience were remotely related to our subjects of interest were studying unions, collective bargaining, wages, etc. Columbia University's Conservation of Human Resources, under Dr. Eli Ginzberg's direction, was the only on-going institution concerned with labor market issues relevant to our mission.

In examining the early proposals submitted to our office we concluded that we were suffering from a "tired blood" syndrome in that so few young researchers appeared to be interested in studying the issues which concerned us. In an effort to attract new researchers we first broadcast, through a variety of channels, our interest in supporting research on a specified list of employment and training problems. We were overwhelmed with proposals that seemed to come primarily from persons or organizations with little or no research background.

Dr. Ginzberg, in discussing our experience with us, suggested that we produce our own experts. This led us to start a doctoral dissertation program which proved to be one of our most significant long term accomplishments. Many of the country's leading social scientists now working on employment and training issues were able to get their Ph.D.s through this program.[4]

During the early years we primarily used unsolicited proposals and sole source awards in order to secure research performers. We often sought out specialists who were studying subjects relevant to our program needs. Once our budget increased and we could be involved in more costly research and development efforts, we made greater use of Requests for Proposals (RFPs). We tried, however, to maintain a balance between unsolicited proposals and RFPs because we always wanted to have access to the talents of the academic community. RFP procurements appeared to attract few college professors because they were not able to match the grantsmanship capability of the consulting firms.

About two-thirds of the proposals submitted were rejected. Ninety percent of the unsolicited proposals were turned down. We were constantly winnowing not only the proposals but also the researchers. We had to distinguish between scholars who appeared to be only concerned with furthering their disciplines and those who were genuinely interested in social and economic problems. Many of the researchers who were caught in the publish or perish syndrome submitted proposals that were more directed toward furthering their reputations than in making contributions to our knowledge about the social and economic issues identified in MDTA. We found very few scholars or consulting organizations able to assist us in getting research findings utilized or interested in following through in having their studies used for policy decisions.

There was, and still is, a real shortage of social scientists capable of combining their research background with the very practical real world problems of organizing and conducting experimental and demonstration projects with rigorous research designs. Few, if any, of our training institutions appear to have recognized the need for researchers who can both apply scientific research methods and carry out the necessary nitty-gritty chores required for establishing small-scale experimental and demonstration projects which can tell policymakers whether large-scale programs are feasible or desirable.

One of the key factors affecting the success or failure of a research and development program is the review process. Before we made a decision on which review method to use, we consulted with several research offices in federal agencies. After prolonged and frank discussions with some of the administrators who established the National Institutes of Health (NIH) we decided *not* to use peer review of proposals by nongovernmental panels of experts. Although this system was in use at NIH, we were advised that if they were starting all over again, some of these administrators would no longer use this system. Their view was that peer review too often ends up in an "old boy" system of mutual back-scratching. They also believed that new young researchers and innovators found it more difficult to break into the funding circle controlled by more established scientists. We settled on a review system which included staff assessment and extensive examination by specialists in the federal government as well as by nongovernmental experts.

No honest account of a research and development administrator's reflections could possibly exclude reference to the real world of political pressures that pervade the very air of Washington. Let me start with the flat assertion that I was always surprised by how little pressure was exerted on us to fund performers who came through the political route. Ninety-nine percent of the products we funded were based on our decisions rather than those imposed by political appointees. If there is credit or blame to be given for success or failure of this particular research and development effort, it should be directed to the career staff who administered the program.

This does not say that efforts were not made to secure funding through the political route. Most of these proposals were fended off by our normal review process. Remember that our office rejected at least 90 percent of unsolicited proposals. Upon occasion, in order to take heat off career employees, we would convene ad hoc panels of well-known social scientists to review a proposal in which either the White House or a congressman had indicated more than casual interest. After this review, we were usually able to inform the applicants and their sponsors how a panel of nationally known experts had voted.

There seemed to be little difference in the amount of pressure exerted by either of the two major parties. We learned that, for the most part, bona fide researchers did not apply for funding through the political route. We identified pressure as proposals forwarded by the White House or sent to us by senators or representatives. It was relatively easy to distinguish between proposals that were transmitted as a matter of routine courtesy to constituents from those in which there was a genuine interest.

Congressional oversight of our program was minimal. The Office of Management and Budget's annual review was primarily an educational activity to apprise the examiners and analysts of our findings and major funding. We had two experiences with the General Accounting Office (GAO). In the first instance we were advised that GAO was prepared to launch a major study of how we used our research products.

After spending two hours explaining that we had established a separate division just to concentrate on the utilization of research and development findings and specifying how this activity was being conducted, the representatives of GAO quietly left and never returned. We were visited a second time by the GAO for an examination of our procurement activities. After an exhaustive survey they tapped us on the wrist by pointing out that some of our files were incomplete in that all necessary documents were not immediately available.

We had one experience with the donor of the Golden Fleece Award. For several years we had been conducting a series of studies and small-scale research demonstration projects to determine whether income assistance might reduce recidivism among ex-offenders. We were interested in the employment experience of ex-offenders because one out of two clients in the manpower programs had either arrest or incarceration records. Local, state and federal correctional institutions were releasing prisoners to the outside world with sums of money that varied from 25 cents to $50 or just a suit of clothes. Our earliest research indicated that most ex-offenders would have to depend on the weak reed of friends or relatives for income support after they left prison.

After years of careful documentation and review of our initial review and experimental and demonstration efforts by a panel of penologists, we decided to conduct an experiment in Georgia and Texas to determine whether unemployment insurance might reduce the recidivism rate of released prisoners. Shortly after the project began a Georgia newspaperman called Senator Proxmire's office to advise a member of his staff that the Department of Labor was funding a project which gave money to "pimps, rapists and murderers." We were immediately called and asked to submit a description of our project to the Senator.

We forwarded the requested material which described the experimental design, our years of study, and the rationale for the work. We also pointed out that Dr. Peter Rossi, former president of the American Sociological Association, was chief researcher and that the project was being supervised by the American Bar Association. We waited a few days before calling the Senator's assistant, who was most pleasant to us. He complimented us so highly on our rigorous design and professional research that I was moved to ask whether the Senator might want to consider the project for a Diamond Fleece Award as an exemplary government research project. I was told that I was overstepping my bounds and the conversation was abruptly terminated. That was the last I heard from this type of senatorial oversight.

To summarize our external environment, we created a research community of scholars interested in employment and training issues by launching a doctoral dissertation program which proved to be very helpful in encouraging young scholars to study labor market operations. We tried to maintain a balanced procurement process which left the door open so that we were exposed to new and innovative ideas and researchers. We were constantly searching for researchers who were concerned with the impact of their studies on policy issues. We found very few social scientists who could develop a good research design and translate it into a real world experimental or demonstration project. Apparently, our proposal review process effectively minimized political pressure on career employees.

Research Strategy

The primary motive for passage of the Manpower Act was to provide training and retraining in order to ameliorate the effects of automation and technological changes on unemployed workers who previously had a relatively strong attachment to the labor market. These were the white blue-collar workers whom Senator Kennedy had seen during his presidential campaign in West Virginia. In addition to automation, the act directed us to discover why shortages of qualified personnel existed even during periods of high unemployment. We were also expected to identify areas of current and prospective manpower shortages and to report on occupations which promised reasonable expectations of employment and on-the-job training opportunities for trainees who participated in government sponsored training programs.

Shortly after the legislation was passed, students of labor market changes noted that despite all of the talk about automation, unemployment was declining and the number of employed workers was increasing. Between 1962 and 1965, the rate of unemployment dropped from 5.5 to 4.5 percent and employment rose by 4.3 million from 66.7 to 71.0 million. Other researchers also reported that the automation of the early and mid-1960s was not about to wipe out millions of jobs and leave us with mechanized factories that would displace millions of workers.

Some students of the American economy alerted the country to the growing number of unskilled and poorly educated workers who could benefit from training and retraining. Our office conducted a survey for President Kennedy's Task Force on Manpower Conservation which was published with the nostalgic title of *One-Third of a Nation.* This report documented that one-half of the young men called for preinduction examination under Selective Service were found unqualified for military service.[5] Fully one-third of the age group did not meet the required standards of health and education. Our survey also showed that a major proportion of these young men were the products of poverty that they inherited from their parents and unless the skills of the rejectees were upgraded, these young men would face a lifetime of recurrent unemployment.

The labor force data, White House memoranda, popular articles and books on poverty, *One-Third of a Nation,* all contributed to a major shift in manpower policy from concentration on workers displaced by automation to economically disadvantaged workers and youths. By the end of the Kennedy Administration and the beginning of the Johnson presidency, manpower policy had moved to the war on poverty.

Developing a meaningful and coherent research strategy for a social science program in a federal agency proved to be a real challenge. Annual budgets, a constantly shifting group of political appointees, changes in priorities and the need of policymakers for immediate answers to complex issues made it difficult to plan for a long term program. We were acutely aware that social science research was more capable of providing information than solutions to complex and deep-rooted economic and social problems. For this reason, we could not over promise results to political managers who wanted clear cut unambiguous research findings which could be used for making decisions.

In order to survive, our research strategy called for two levels of projects. Realistically, we knew that a research organization in a mission-oriented federal agency must put aside a certain proportion of its resources for what can be described as "quick and dirty" research. This research was designed to give political appointees and other administrators information that could be used for making current policy decisions.

The second type of research, which we believed was more suitable to social science research capabilities, was directed toward the cumulative acquisition of information about major employment and training problems. One of the most important lessons we learned in administering the research and development programs is that ad hoc and unrelated projects do not, for the most part, have as great an impact as cumulative research on major social and economic issues. Those of us who started ETA's research and development program soon came to the realization that social science research is more comparable to the slow, long term accumulation of information about cancer than the discovery and immediate application of the Salk vaccine leading to the sudden disappearance of infantile paralysis.

The best example of an investment in basic and long term research was our support for a national longitudinal survey of 20,000 workers which began in the mid-1960s and is still continuing in 1984. The data of the labor market experience of 20,000 workers representing the American labor force in four broad age categories are collected by the Census Bureau. The National Longitudinal Survey (NLS) data include information on employment and unemployment experience, occupational training, aspirations, education, health, family backgrounds and exposure to counseling. The cumulative data base of the NLS is now one of the nation's most important sources of information on the work experience of American workers. The findings of the NLS have had an impact on legislation, programs and policy decisions. They have been analyzed and used by scholars in hundreds of articles, monographs and books.

Another example of long term support was the study of the effects of occupational licensing on the employment opportunities of nonprofessional workers.[6] After a 1967 survey of state and local licensing laws which set the groundwork for further exploration, we embarked on a series of studies and action programs which continued through 1980. In order to remove the barriers of occupational licensing to employment, we funded the researcher to become a "change agent" to testify before local political leaders and state legislators so that they would know how to draw up more equitable licensing laws. He was consulted extensively by persons concerned with improving occupational licensing laws throughout the United States.

In addition to recognizing the benefits of cumulative research we also learned that the social and economic problems we studied rarely fit neatly into any single social science discipline. Cultural differences, motivation, education, training, health and discrimination were just some of the reasons workers experienced difficulty in the labor market. Our clients had problems which cut across several disciplines rather than any single one. For this reason, we made a deliberate effort to involve sociologists, anthropologists, psychologists, demographers, political scientists, and other social scientists in our research program. We also sought out social scientists who were capable of interdisciplinary research.

In developing our research agenda we followed a practice of specifying major issues and problems. We then asked the research staff to articulate a number of researchable and integrated questions that could be explored and lead to a cumulative base of information. We then sought scholars who may have already started studying some of the issues or tried to persuade others to direct their research skills to the economic and social problems of concern to us. We often followed and supported these peripatetic scholars who were willing to make long term commitments to subjects of interest to the research and development program, as they moved from university to university.

As one would expect, we were originally inundated with proposals to study the effect of automation and technological changes on skill requirements and employment. We had the difficult task of separating charlatans from legitimate researchers. We discovered that there was a cadre of social scientists who were willing to devote their careers to following newspaper headlines in order to study "popular" subjects. Many of these researchers suffered from a reverse of the Midas principle. Wherever there was gold, they wanted to touch it.

After the shift in policy and priorities from automation to concentration on the problems of the economically disadvantaged, we decided that studies of labor market operations would be the basic foundation of our research strategy. We then went on to support research that examined institutional obstacles that some workers faced in entering and maneuvering through the labor market. In addition to studies of employers' hiring practices, occupational licensing and job market information, we supported research which examined the special employment problems of blacks, Hispanics, women, youth, older workers, ex-offenders and migrant workers.

In order to broaden the research strategy, some of the country's leading social scientists were first invited to join a committee to advise the research office on future program directions. Because members came from different disciplines, it was sometimes difficult to secure agreement on subjects for studies or research methodologies. Eventually, the committee was discontinued and greater dependence was placed on staff-originated proposals, unsolicited proposals and suggestions forwarded by the operating, planning and policy staffs.

As a result of the merger, in 1970, of the Office of Special Manpower Projects and the research office, the new annual research and development budget increased from $2.8 to $13.0 million. This larger budget enabled the office to now support experimental and demonstration projects in addition to conventional research. We hoped that these small scale experimental and demonstration projects could now be used to test the feasibility of new concepts and programs before moving to large national efforts.

The Office of Special Manpower Projects originally was assigned to support experimental and demonstration efforts during the 1960s. These projects were operated primarily as catalysts for social action, with the formal generation of information and insight regarding operational problems as an important, but subsidiary, concern. The new combined Office of Research and Development (ORD) adopted a policy that research had to be an integral component of all experimental and demonstration projects. The operators of experimental and demonstration projects who were primarily oriented to provide services to clients also had to be persuaded to cooperate with researchers who were studying their programs.

We soon discovered that "carrying out any social experiment successfully is a managerial tour de force. . . ."[7] Our largest investment in a demonstration research project with a randomized experimental control group was *Supported Work* which was a 5-year effort to test whether individuals with severe employment problems could be made employable by exposing them to a controlled work experience. The demonstration research project proved most effective in preparing for employment a substantial number of women who had been on welfare (AFDC) for many years. The program also had an impact on a significant segment of the study's ex-addict population. There was only a marginal effect on ex-offenders who did not show less criminal behavior and whose rate of employment and earnings were only slightly better than a control group of ex-offenders. Neither was there any long term positive results for the youths in the demonstration project.

A second random experimental control project, which coincidentally also offered services to female heads of households in AFDC, involved an effort to move women on welfare from the secondary to the primary labor market so that they could become self-supporting. Welfare mothers were entered in selected training institutions that offered tightly structured instructional formats, remedial education and a proven record of placing graduates in expanding occupations with starting wages of more than $9,000 per year. We learned that it was possible to make a certain proportion of women on welfare self-supporting. The results indicated that a significant investment in training, remedial education and supportive services could overcome the destructiveness of poverty, poor education and discrimination for some women on AFDC.[8]

In summing up our experience in developing and maintaining a research strategy in a mission-oriented federal agency, it is worth noting that missions are subject to change even without new legislation. For example, the concept of "economically disadvantaged" was not articulated in the laws controlling our programs until the Comprehensive Employment and Training Act (CETA) of 1973. The spillover of the war against poverty, which pervaded the government during the 1960s, contributed to the change of the direction of the employment and training program.

As indicated earlier, administrators of federal research and development programs, if they are to survive, must be responsive to the immediate needs of political appointees and be prepared to support short term research that might be useful for current policy decisions. Although cumulative, long term information-building research seems to provide more valid findings than some ad hoc research, it is far more difficult to introduce and maintain in a federal environment oriented to annual budgets and quick and easy solutions of enormously complex problems.

The deep-rooted causes of unemployment, discrimination and other factors handicapping workers rarely match single social science research disciplines. For this reason, interdisciplinary research efforts and more cooperation among federal agencies are needed to explore social and economic problems assigned to the government. Finally, in spite of the difficulties in managing experimental and demonstration projects and their other limitations, greater effort should be made to test small scale exploratory projects before launching major national large scale programs.

Policy: The Evanescent Goal

Government decisions affecting policies or courses of action are generally not traceable to a clearly demarcated event. Instead, they are more likely to be part of a slow, inefficient and haphazard process. Unfortunately, research findings are rarely available at the exact moment they are needed in making policy decisions. Furthermore, many research studies produce ambiguous results at a time when a decision-maker seeks clear-cut findings. Because of timing and ambiguity problems, social science research can primarily contribute enlightenment rather than solutions to the policymaking process. Notwithstanding the inherent difficulties associated with social research, administrators of federal research and development programs are regularly challenged by newly appointed political officeholders with the question, "What impact has your program had on policy?"

In assessing the effect of ETA's research and development program on policy decisions, it is well to keep in mind that between 1962 and 1980, the Department of Labor had eight secretaries and five assistant secretaries responsible for administering employment and training programs. One could reply to the previous question with another question, "Whose policy?" Not only did the top personnel change quite often, but so did the policy direction of the program. As noted earlier, program concentration shifted from workers affected by automation to economically disadvantaged workers. The system of delivery of services changed drastically between MDTA and CETA from centralized delivery to decentralization. New deliverers of service known as Prime Sponsors were introduced. In addition, public employment programs were introduced in the 1973 legislation and the responsibility for providing services to special target groups such as youth, offenders, persons of limited English-speaking ability and older workers was assigned to the federal government.

The combination of the number of political appointees, their rapid turnover and short term orientation as well as major shifts in priorities and philosophy compounded the job of a research administrator interested in developing a coherent, cumulative, long term program that could contribute to policy decisions. We soon learned that most political appointees are not interested in funding projects that will deliver findings long after they have left office.

Our experience in trying to introduce policy issues in the *President's Manpower Report* (also known as the *Employment and Training Report of the President*) is worth noting. We were constantly criticized because this report, which was our responsibility, was not used as a vehicle for introducing new significant policy issues. In response to this criticism, we attempted to introduce policy issues which we thought could be agreed upon by the review process. We discovered that unilaterally originated policy was shot down in the extensive interagency review process. Each reviewer refused to accept responsibility for approving a policy that had not been previously agreed upon by his political superior. It became obvious that this was the wrong way to introduce policy issues. In order to bring new employment and training policy issues to the fore it would have been first necessary to secure agreement from cabinet officers and then use the report route. We decided that it was not worth the time and effort and were content to let the report simply describe programs and provide data on labor force, employment and unemployment, hours, earnings and turnover.

In addition to a very active publishing program which produced dozens of monographs summarizing what we learned from research and development projects, we devised several tactics for bringing current research findings to the attention of policymakers so that they could be used in the decision-making process. One device which proved to be quite effective was to ask researchers to make personal presentations to people in policy positions. During the height of the U.S.

debate on the possible use of public service jobs in employment and training programs, one of our researchers reported
to the Secretary of Labor on a study of the effect of public
service programs on unemployment in several European
countries. Another researcher discussed with an assistant
secretary the findings of a study of the employment problems of black professional women in southern cities. A
Secretary of Labor heard a detailed report on the results of a
long term study of income assistance to ex-offenders. This
procedure effectively kept policymakers current with the
latest research findings.

Executive summaries of the results of research and
development projects relevant to their work or interest were
distributed regularly to policymakers in the Department of
Labor, executives in other federal agencies, senators and
representatives, and key staff members on the Hill. Interest
groups and leaders of public opinion in the public and
private sectors were sent selected research and development
reports. Monographs and reports were sent to the research
community. For example, Peter B. Doeringer and Michael J.
Piore's work on the dual labor market theory was published
as an ETA monograph and given wide distribution. In
recognition of the cumulative nature of social science
research, we published syntheses of several reports on the
same general subject area.

The products of the research office probably had their
greatest impact on legislation. We were able to directly trace
the findings of research studies on amendments to the
original Manpower Act. Reference to certain target groups
and concepts introduced in the CETA legislation can be trac-
ed back to research and development findings. Our location
in the Office of Policy, Evaluation and Research gave us
easy access to staff members who were developing policy
statements or preparing legislation. They used our research
reports in developing new legislative proposals.

As suggested earlier, it is almost impossible to determine which research results help to shape policy decisions. Nor is it possible to predict, in advance, what impact research findings will have on policy. The single research study funded by the Office of Research and Development, which probably had the greatest immediate and traceable impact on public and private policy was a modestly funded study of the reasons for the low level of black participation in apprenticeship programs.[9]

The findings of this study, which documented the reasons why so few blacks were in apprenticeship and described the methods used to bar their entry, resulted in a sharp and immediate redirection of the program of the Bureau of Apprenticeship and Training and changed the apprenticeship selection system of unions and employers. The results were used by public agencies and private interest groups concerned with equal employment opportunities. Based on this study, the Department of Labor funded action programs designed to assist minorities in entering apprenticeship programs. The findings and their use in programs of this research project were probably the primary reason for the large increase of black participation in apprenticeship programs during the 1960s and 1970s.

Apparently, an unusual combination of factors contributed to the acceptance and immediate use of this study of the apprenticeship system. The right questions were evidently asked at a time in history when there was a receptive audience of public and private policymakers who were willing to act on the research findings. It coincided with a civil rights movement that was seeking targets. No one could have predicted in advance that this small research project would have had such a far-reaching impact on policy. Certainly, one cannot generalize about policy-oriented research based on this and hundreds of other projects. The combination of levels of funding, subjects studied, questions asked, the receptivity of policymakers, timing and the temper of the times are not too helpful in anticipating the impact of research on policy.

When the research program was 10 years old, the Department of Labor asked the National Academy of Sciences-National Research Council to establish a committee to review, assess and make recommendations regarding the manpower research and development program. Among the topics covered by the committee was the "relevance of the Department's R&D efforts to . . . influence . . . the development of national manpower and related policies and programs. . . ."[10] After analyzing a sample of almost 1,000 projects funded by the Office of Research and Development between 1963 and 1975, commissioning papers on specific aspects of the ORD program and conducting 375 interviews, the committee concluded that the "manpower R&D program has made a number of outstanding contributions to policy. . . ."[11]

The committee reported that ORD had been instrumental in identifying and exploring the complexities of manpower problems. It referred specifically to our work on job vacancies, projections of future manpower requirements, the nature and extent of occupational training of the nation's labor force, the spatial and occupational distribution of unemployment and underemployment and the employment experience of minority workers and the economically and socially disadvantaged. Studies of labor market deficiencies, including the adverse effects of occupational licensing, employment discrimination and the development of new theories to illuminate complexities of labor market operations were also cited as examples of research and development projects influencing policy and programs. The committee noted the realities of the research office's existence in an operationally oriented federal department subject to frequent shifts in policy. As a result of the committee's interviews, it found only scant acceptance among department officials "of the need for comprehensive, extended efforts aimed at better understanding fundamental and persistent manpower problems."[12]

To summarize our experience in policy-oriented research, we would conclude that the design of a social science research program which can be useful to policymakers in a mission-oriented agency is probably the greatest challenge faced by research administrators. The turnover of political appointees, many of whom take government positions with preconceived biases and special agendas, the general lack of interest in long term research and frequent changes in priorities and legislation all reduce the potential contribution of social research to the policymaking process. In spite of these difficulties, a research administrator must constantly explore ways of bringing valid research findings to the attention of decisionmakers.

Disappointments and Accomplishments

In reviewing 18 years of experience as an administrator of a federal research and development program, I should like to first comment on some of my disappointments. I fear that little can be done about my negative conclusions.

Let me again start with the caveat that my comments on political leadership apply to both political parties. The Department of Labor was quite fortunate in being administered by political appointees between 1962 and 1980 who, for the most part, if not interested in social science research at least tolerated it. Unfortunately, our political system often brings appointees into the government who not only know very little about the programs they are to administer but who are unable to use social science research findings in making policy decisions. Communicating the objective results of research findings to some political appointees was sometimes a futile exercise. I see little likelihood in the foreseeable future that presidents will ever make selections of political appointees on the basis of their program knowledge or their ability to use research findings.

My second major disappointment was with the social science research community. Most of the social scientists who applied for research funding to the Office of Research and Development seemed to be unaware that they were approaching a research organization in a mission-oriented agency. Many of them never took the time to read the law under which we operated.

Our graduate educational system seems to turn out too many researchers who are concerned with methodology, model building, and discipline-oriented research that is of little use to those concerned with the nation's economic and social problems. Our educational system seems to destroy whatever creativity or innovativeness students may have before they become researchers. Too many social scientists do not recognize that social research is cumulative and often requires long term commitment on the part of the researcher. Again, as with political appointees, I foresee little possibility in the near future of improvement in the training of social scientists. Graduate schools will continue to produce too many narrow discipline-oriented researchers, most of whom will have little interest in applying their research skills to real world problems.

What did we accomplish in 18 years of the research and development program?

In order to attempt to answer this question I refer to a 16-year compilation of research and development projects.[13] I was first struck by the enormous diversity of our interests. Our projects covered almost every subject in the employment and training field. Second, although we made considerable investments in applied program research, we still managed to support basic research. Third, we funded a large number of assessment and evaluation projects which provided policymakers with objective data on the effectiveness of Department of Labor programs. If one wanted to get information to criticize DOL's work, one simply could turn to the research findings of projects funded by a neutral, professional social science research program conducted by a federal agency. Fourth, the true meaning of cumulative research became apparent in tracing projects that slowly built on previous research findings. Our studies of illegal immigrants, discrimination, occupational licensing, employment problems of ex-offenders, barriers to employment and other labor market operation projects were supported over 10-year periods. The continuity of support and the commitment of researchers to particular subject areas effectively build a bank of information on important social and economic problems. Fifth, our intensive concentration on certain issues is certainly impressive. For example, our early research predicted that important social and economic developments were changing the work pattern and life style of American women.

During the first 16 years of the program, some 128 projects were funded to examine the work and employment problems of women workers. The subjects studied ranged from women in nontraditional blue-collar jobs, maternity leave benefits, child care arrangements of working mothers, labor force mobility of women, the effects of marriage and divorce on labor force participation, fertility and career patterns, dual careers, minority women in white-collar jobs, female heads of families, marital status and occupational mobility of women, econometric analysis of the part-time labor market for women and career patterns of women physicians. These research studies combined with experimental and developmental projects designed to break new ground for women in the labor market can be considered a major accomplishment of the program.

As noted earlier, our research and development work contributed to a broader understanding of the employment problems of the economically disadvantaged of our society. Exploratory studies of unemployment in the ghetto changed the data collection system of BLS and the Census Bureau. A series of studies of the employment problems of ex-offenders led to changes in questions on job application forms of state and local government about arrest records. Much of our work was translated into legislative amendments and the introduction of new concepts in legislation.

The development and continuing support of the National Longitudinal Surveys has provided the country with new information about the employment experience of our workforce, the effect of health on work and retirement, labor force participation of women, discrimination, attitudes toward work and the result of inadequate labor market knowledge on the earnings and careers of minority youth. The longitudinal nature of these surveys has given us, for the first time, predictive tools and a broader understanding of how social and cultural changes affect work patterns.

Our efforts to improve the methodologies used to assess social programs should provide more valid findings for the use of policymakers. In my view, the emphasis we placed on the use of random assignments, control groups, cost accounting, adequate samples and the professional management of experimental and demonstration projects contributed to the improvement of the state of art of experimental and demonstration projects. We believe that the Supported Work model established a landmark for future research demonstration projects.

The grant and institutional support programs played a central role in increasing the number and improving the quality of researchers active in the field of employment and training. Well over 500 recipients of grants completed their doctorates. The institutional grant program, which funded undergraduate study and self-directed faculty research helped increase academically-based research centers.

One final reflection: the management of a program involving thousands of projects and millions of dollars of federal funds is obviously not a one-person job. The quality and effectiveness of the research and development program depended on the small number of career servants who conducted the day-to-day operations of soliciting, developing and reviewing proposals, handling the onerous details associated with government contracts and grants, monitoring projects and planning utilization strategy. These employees had to combine practical managerial skill with a professional knowledge of the social sciences. Praising government employees is not a popular pastime in Washington in 1984. But I would be remiss if I did not pay tribute to the professionalism, conscientiousness and dedication of the federal employees who contributed to the success of the Employment and Training Administration's research and development program.

Washington is noted for the short term careers of political appointees who leave few lasting reminders of their ephemeral fame. In contrast, the civil servants who participated in ETA's research and development program can rest assured that they have left a lasting legacy of knowledge and information which has had and will continue to have an impact on some of this country's most complex social and economic problems.

NOTES

1. Public Law 87-415, *The Manpower Development and Training Act of 1962,* 87th Congress, March 15, 1962, Title I, Section 102, p. 2.

2. The original group assigned to work on MDTA under Dr. Wolfbein, who was a deputy to the Secretary of Labor, consisted of Margaret Thomas, Joseph (Jerry) Zeisel, Earl Klein and the author of these reflections.

3. U.S. Department of Labor, *Formal Occupational Training of Adult Workers,* Manpower/Automation Research Monograph No. 2, 1964.

4. Some of the recipients of the doctoral awards still working on problems of employment and training include Robert J. Flanagan, Robert Taggart III, Sharon P. Smith, Leonard J. Hausman, Ronald L. Oaxaca,

James L. Medoff, Peter Doeringer, James J. Heckman, Collette H. Moser, Richard B. Freeman, Daniel Quinn Mills, Robert J. Lerman, Frank Mott, Ronald G. Ehrenberg, Kenneth I. Wolpin, Bennett Harrison, Thomas A. Barocci, Harriet Zellner and Francine O. Blau.

5. The President's Task Force on Manpower Conservation, *One-Third of a Nation: A Report on Young Men Found Unqualified for Military Service,* January 1, 1964.

6. Benjamin Shonberg, Barbara F. Essen, and Daniel H. Kruger, *Occupational Licensing: Practices and Policies* (Washington, DC: Public Affairs Press, 1972).

7. Alice M. Rivlin, "How Can Experiments Be More Useful?" *The American Economic Review* 64, No. 2 (May 1974), pp. 346-53.

8. Considerable credit for the excellent management of the Supported Work Project and the educational project for women on welfare should be given to Fritz Kramer and Gordon Berlin, two dedicated staff members of the Office of Research and Development, who shepherded the projects from origin to conclusion.

9. F. Ray Marshall and Vernon M. Briggs, Jr., *The Negro and Apprenticeship* (Baltimore: The Johns Hopkins University Press, 1967).

10. National Academy of Sciences, *Knowledge and Policy in Manpower* (Washington, DC, 1975), p. iv.

11. Ibid., p. 13.

12. Ibid., p. 25.

13. U.S. Department of Labor, Employment and Training Administration, *Research and Development: A 16-Year Compendium (1963-78),* Washington, DC, 1979.

Policy Lessons
From Three
Labor Market Experiments

Gary Burtless
Robert H. Haveman

Social experimentation began in earnest when the New Jersey negative income tax experiment was launched in 1967. For the next 14 years, government agencies and philanthropic organizations sponsored a wide variety of experiments and demonstrations involving innovations in social policy; none were more important than those concerning the controversial income support-work issue. In this paper we consider three of the most important social policy experiments: the Seattle-Denver Income Maintenance Experiment, the National Supported Work Demonstration, and the Employment Opportunity Pilot Project. These projects have yielded findings of broad significance to social policy, though the significance of their findings is only dimly perceived by policymakers and interested scholars. Our purpose in this review is to briefly describe the experiments and state the main policy conclusions that can be drawn from them. In our final section, we will discuss some conclusions about the effects and value of social experiments in general.

105

The Seattle-Denver Experiment

The Seattle-Denver experiment was the largest and most comprehensive of the Negative Income Tax (NIT) experiments. It was begun in Seattle in 1970 and in Denver in 1971 under contracts between the States of Washington and Colorado and the U.S. Department of Health, Education, and Welfare. The experiment was administered by Mathematica, a research organization that had already gained valuable administrative experience running the New Jersey experiment. The Stanford Research Institute designed the experiment and was given major responsibility for evaluating it. There is no doubt that the Seattle-Denver experiment was the best run of the NIT experiments, and it was the most thoroughly studied.

Approximately 4800 families were enrolled in the experiment, and families assigned to experimental NIT plans were potentially eligible for payments for a period of either three or five years.[1] To be eligible for enrollment, families had to contain at least one ablebodied, nonaged adult. If only a single adult was present, the family was also required to have one or more dependent children. The sample enrolled in the experiment consisted of lower- and middle-income black, white, and Hispanic families with either one or two parents present. While participation was restricted to residents of Seattle and Denver, families could continue to participate if they moved out of those cities.

The experiment had two main goals, both of which were reflected in its rather elaborate design. The first was to determine the effect of alternative NIT plans on the work behavior of the poor. The second was to test the feasibility and effectiveness of educational vouchers aimed at low-income workers.

The idea behind a negative income tax is fairly well-known and will not be discussed in detail here. In its simplest form, a NIT offers a guaranteed monthly or annual income to a family that has no other income of its own. This amount varies depending on the number of persons in the family and was systematically varied in the experiment to measure the impact of higher or lower income support levels. If a family receives income from nonexperimental sources, such as wage earnings, interest, or public transfers, the monthly NIT payment is reduced in proportion to the amount of other income received. As income from other sources rises, the NIT payment is reduced by an amount determined by the program's tax (or benefit reduction) rate. The tax rate was also systematically varied in the experiment. When income from other sources is sufficiently high that the benefit reduction exactly offsets the income guarantee—at a point known as the break-even—payments under a NIT cease. A NIT's break-even level is algebraically determined by its guarantee and tax rate. As the guarantee level rises, the break-even also rises; as the tax rate rises, the break-even level declines.

Both theory and common sense suggest that the transfer scheme just described will affect work effort. Those who receive payments will have more income, so the necessity for earned income falls. Because payments are reduced as earned income rises, the reward for work is also affected. Under a benefit reduction rate of 70 percent, for example, a recipient who earns an additional dollar loses $0.70 in NIT benefits, and the net increase in income is only $0.30. The Seattle-Denver experiment tested 11 NIT plans with income guarantees ranging from slightly below to about 40 percent above the poverty threshold and tax rates ranging from about 50 to 70 percent. With this range of tested guarantees and tax rates, the designers hoped to detect the impact of a meaningful array of plans. In retrospect, we can criticize the designers for their conservative assessment of the meaningful range of tax rates. The policy debate since 1977, and especially since 1981, has shown that tax rates in excess of 90 percent or even 100 percent are well within the policy-relevant range.

The random assignment of families or individuals to alternative treatments—or no treatment at all—is what gives social experimentation its unique advantage as a tool for policy analysis. With only a few modest and believable statistical assumptions, it is possible for the analyst of experimental data to establish a definite cause-and-effect relationship between treatment variations and observed outcomes. The direction and precise magnitude of the relationship can be established with known levels of statistical confidence. In the case of the Seattle-Denver experiment, families were randomly assigned to 1 out of the 11 tested NIT plans or to control status. A family enrolled in one of the NIT plans was eligible to receive NIT grants if its income was below the plan's break-even. A family in the control group was not eligible to receive these experimental transfers but could continue to receive any nonexperimental transfers for which it remained eligible. The effect of the NIT plans on work behavior can be reliably determined simply by statistically comparing the work effort of individuals enrolled in the various plans and in the control group.

The work-effort findings from the Seattle-Denver experiment have been summarized in a final report recently issued by the Department of Health and Human Services. Briefly, the report shows that the tested NIT plans caused substantial reductions in labor market activity, particularly for persons enrolled in longer duration (5-year) plans and for women. By "substantial" we mean that prime-aged men reduced their annual hours of work by 9 or 10 percent; that their spouses reduced annual hours by 17 to 20 percent; and that women heading single-parent families reduced annual hours by more than 20 percent—perhaps by as much as 28 to 32 percent.[2] These reported work reductions are large enough to cause alarm among conservatives already opposed to a NIT and even among centrists with no strong opinions about the desirability of a NIT.

Taken by themselves, however, the work reductions just reported have almost nothing to tell us about the desirability or feasibility of enacting a NIT. The work reductions appear to be fairly substantial, but the work disincentive provided by the tested plans was also quite substantial, larger in fact than that which would be provided under most proposed NIT plans. The Seattle-Denver plans tested an average income guarantee of 115 percent of the poverty threshold and a marginal tax averaging only about 50 percent. In addition, the experiment provided rebates for state, federal, and FICA taxes on earned income. About 80 percent of enrolled families faced a break-even level that was more than one-and-a-half times the poverty threshold, and 50 percent faced a break-even more than twice the poverty level (that is, above $19,600 for a family of four in 1982 dollars). By contrast, the combined income guarantee provided by AFDC and food stamps is now below the poverty level in most states, and the *break-even* level for AFDC is below the poverty level in all but 15 states.[3]

Even so, the labor supply findings from Seattle-Denver were considered sufficiently important to affect the welfare reform proposals submitted by the Carter Administration.[4] The reason was quite simple. The results showed quite convincingly that the work incentive provided by a NIT's low marginal tax rate was more than offset by the work disincentive effects caused by higher overall transfers. For example, simulations based upon the Seattle-Denver results demonstrated that replacement of the current welfare and food stamp programs with a national NIT that has a guarantee equal to three-quarters of the poverty line and a marginal tax rate of 50 percent would reduce aggregate labor supply in two-parent families by about 1 percent. Labor supply in two-parent families with annual incomes below $5,000 would be reduced by more than 8 percent.[5] Although we do not find these estimates discouraging by themselves, they contain an implication that is dispiriting to policymakers who wish to simultaneously support incomes and increase the self-reliance of needy families. According to the Seattle-Denver estimates, under the NIT plan just described it would cost the government $1.79 in transfer outlays to raise the net income of poor two-parent families by $1.00. In other words, 44 percent of the net program costs of the NIT would be "consumed" by breadwinners in the form of leisure. (The net program cost of the NIT is the amount by which NIT transfers exceed those now paid under the welfare and food stamp programs.)

Another important—though at first glance, per-verse—result from the experiment was that lowering work incentives in transfer programs by raising their marginal tax rates (holding the guarantee constant) serves to *increase* aggregate work effort. For example, if the tax rate in the NIT just described were raised from 50 to 70 percent, the Seattle-Denver results indicated that aggregate work effort would rise by 1 percent.[6] The result is attributable to the fact that while increases in marginal tax rates may indeed reduce the work effort of continued transfer recipients, that effect is more than outweighed by the *increases* in work effort that occur among those who lose benefits altogether. (Recall that a rise in the marginal tax rate with a constant guarantee causes a fall in the break-even and hence a reduction in the number of transfer recipients.)

If one's sole objective is to increase work effort, the recent increases in AFDC tax rates might conceivably be justified by findings of the Seattle-Denver experiment.[7] This conclusion, however, rests on the premise that the main objective of transfer policy is to encourage work effort. In fact, the primary objective of a NIT is to protect the living standards of people who would otherwise be destitute, and to do so in an equitable and efficient way. The contribution of the NIT program to this objective, it should be noted, has received only slight attention in the hundreds of research reports filed on the NIT experiments. This in spite of the fact that the tested NIT plans were potentially quite effective in attaining that goal. Nevertheless, the Seattle-Denver experiment has played the useful role of overturning the notion, especially popular among economists and idealistic reformers, that lower marginal tax rates are automatically associated with a greater stimulus to work.

The second objective of the experiment was to test the effectiveness of issuing education and training vouchers to low-income breadwinners. Families in the experiment were randomly assigned to one of three employment-training programs or to control status.[8] All three of the labor market programs provided a structured course of manpower counseling to help participants decide on an appropriate strategy of employment, education, and training. This course was voluntary, informational in content, and nondirective (that is, participants were not encouraged to pursue any particular course of action). One of the tested programs offered no service beyond this counseling. The other two offered subsidies to pay for some or all of the direct costs of schooling or training.[9] Two levels of voucher subsidy were tested. In the more generous plan, 100 percent of direct training costs were reimbursed by the experiment. In the other plan, only 50 percent of costs were reimbursed. Participants could use their vouchers to pay for any education or training they chose, so long as it was at least tangentially related to improving their future job prospects.

The purpose of the vouchers was to encourage eligible breadwinners to invest in worthwhile training and education, which according to human capital theory should have improved participants' employability and future earnings. Participation in the program was reasonably high. About one-fifth of family heads in two-parent families used the 50 percent vouchers, and over one-third used the 100 percent vouchers. About one-third of single mothers eligible for the 50 percent vouchers used them, as did nearly one-half of those eligible for the 100 percent vouchers. Not surprisingly, much of the subsidy went to pay for schooling that would have been obtained in the absence of the program. Most of the subsidies paid for attendance in formal academic programs, such as those run by community colleges, rather than for technical training. The more generous subsidy program succeeded in encouraging extra investment in formal schooling, with the rise averaging about one-half an academic quarter among men eligible for the subsidies and about one to one-and-one-half extra quarters among eligible women.[10]

The interesting finding from this experiment is the complete lack of evidence that the increased investment in schooling by participants led to any pay-off in the job market. On the contrary, persons eligible for vouchers—in comparison to control-group members—suffered short term reductions in wage rates, earnings, and employment during the initial phase of their eligibility. And they never showed consistent earnings gains over the entire 6-year span for which information is available, a period which includes a fairly lengthy spell in which participants had completed their schooling.[11] One explanation for this result is that the vouchers induced significant short term reductions in work effort and work intensity by subsidizing an alternative use of time—enrollment in formal schooling. After the training was completed, participants' earnings failed to rise above the level observed in the control group because of the amount and character of extra schooling obtained. The amount of extra schooling was on average very small, and it was apparently not particularly relevant to the participants' labor market situation. A second explanation concerns the effect of a rather poor and generally deteriorating labor market on the earnings potential of those who reduce (or cease) their work in order to obtain additional schooling. In such a labor market, the returns to work experience and job-keeping may be in excess of those to increased schooling. It is difficult to make training pay off if there are few jobs available.

Employment and training programs for the poor are sometimes criticized for being too rigid, too bureaucratic, too paternalistic, and too insensitive to the special needs of different clients. The experimental test of manpower vouchers in Seattle and Denver shows that completely decentralized decisionmaking, an approach often advocated by economists, may not be an effective substitute for our present arrangements, at least in the face of low labor demand. When given the resources and freedom to choose their own training strategy, low-income breadwinners appear to be no better at selecting a winning strategy than are the administrators and training specialists who now run training and employment programs.

The National Supported Work Demonstration

The 1970's commitment to assist hard-to-employ workers in finding jobs is perhaps best illustrated by the Supported Work Program. The program was a research and demonstration program, rather than a comprehensive employment program. It began in 1975 and was, from its inception, scheduled to last five years. Its basic objective was to provide individuals who had severe employment problems with work experience of about one year. The work experience was provided under conditions of gradually increasing demands, close supervision, and work in association with a crew of peers. The guiding principle of the demonstration was that ". . . by participating in the program, a significant number of people who are severely handicapped for employment may be able to join the labor force and do productive work, cease engaging in socially destructive or dependent behavior, and become self-supporting members of society."[12]

Four groups of employment-handicapped workers were eligible for the program: female long term recipients of AFDC, convicts recently released from prison, former drug addicts, and young school dropouts who often had a delinquency record. Fifteen sites were chosen for the program. While each site was given responsibility for defining the type of work on which it would focus and the source of local funds on which it would draw, the entire program had a common research-evaluation emphasis. Hence, a variety of factors were standardized across the 15 sites. These included the basic program design of low supervisor-participant ratios, steadily increasing standards of attendance, punctuality, and productivity, crew work and peer group support, and common eligibility criteria, wage rates, and employment duration. Like the Seattle-Denver experiment, the Supported Work Demonstration used a rigorous experimental design involving the random assignment of applicants to experimental (participant) and control (nonparticipant comparison) groups. We can therefore place substantial confidence in the demonstration's findings.

Over its 5-year life, the demonstration provided services to over 10,000 persons, although at any point in time the number of participants at any site was limited to 300. The evaluation of the demonstration was based on interviews with 3,214 participants and 3,402 controls. Each person in the research sample was interviewed prior to participation and given up to four additional interviews at 9-month intervals.

The participants suffered severe employment handicaps. Fewer than one-third had graduated from high school, most were black or Hispanic, fewer than one-quarter were married, the number weeks worked in the year prior to enrollment averaged six or seven, and (except for the female welfare group) arrest rates ranged from 54 to 100 percent. The work provided varied across sites, but included home rehabilitation, recapping tires, building furniture, and operating day care centers. Some program outputs were sold in the market in order to raise revenues for the program.

The program performance of the four enrolled groups varied considerably. Supported Work proved most effective in preparing the welfare women who had least work experience for gainful employment. It also had a significant impact on the ex-addict group. For the ex-offender group, the results were marginal and not statistically significant, while no long term positive results were found for the group of young dropouts. Overall, the participants in the program stayed an average of 6.7 months, even though the goal of the demonstration was about 12 months of participation. Thirty percent of the participants were fired because of poor performance; an equivalent number, however, moved on to full-time regular jobs. (The successful transition rate improved steadily over the course of the program.) About 10 percent of the participants (25 percent of the long term welfare women) had to be released after 12 months of participation, because their maximum permissible program stay had been attained. The average cost to the public per recipient was $5,740, but because most participants stayed in the program less than one year, the average cost per service year was over $10,000. This cost declined steadily over the five years of the demonstration and is about the same as the service-year cost in another targeted training program, Job Corps.

The program had a variety of impacts on its participants in areas ranging from drug use and criminal activity to employment behavior and welfare dependency. The AFDC group showed the most consistently positive response to the demonstration. In this group, participation was associated with increases in employment rate, hours worked, and earnings, both during and after the period of program participation. In addition, there was a significant reduction in welfare dependency as well as reduction in the average amount of food stamps and other transfers received. The welfare women helped most by Supported Work tended to be older (between 36 and 44), to be less educated, to have been on welfare for a longer period, and to have little or no prior work experience. At least the last three of these effects would have been difficult to predict prior to the program, and indeed are somewhat surprising.

Among ex-addicts the demonstration raised employment and reduced criminal activity, but failed to have a statistically significant impact on drug use. The main impact on criminal activity seems to have been concentrated in the first 18 months after enrollment in the demonstration. The demonstration's effect on employment probably persisted for longer than that. Ex-convicts in the demonstration do not seem to have been helped as much as the two groups just mentioned. The demonstration did not affect employment, welfare dependence, drug use, or criminal activity after participation ended. Similarly, the youth enrollees were not helped much, if at all, by the program. In this case, however, the evaluators found evidence that the target group was probably more employable than originally believed. At some time during the period of the study, between 80 and 90 percent of youth dropouts in the control group held a job. This level far exceeds the rate of the other three control groups studied, indicating that the youth group was less disadvantaged than the other target groups enrolled.

The Manpower Demonstration Research Corporation and Mathematica conducted a very careful benefit-cost evaluation of the demonstration. They computed the benefits and costs of the program from three different perspectives—that of program participants, that of taxpayers, and that of society as a whole (participants and taxpayers). The social benefits include the output produced by workers in the program, increases in their post-program earnings, reductions in criminal activities, and savings from reduced participation in other public employment, training, or drug treatment programs. The social costs include all program operating costs (excluding transfer payments, however, because these are simply a redistribution of income). The benefit-cost tabulations were based on extrapolations over the typical working life of the participants, with benefits assumed to decay at a rate of 50 percent every five years except among AFDC mothers where no decay rate in benefits is assumed.

The benefit-cost analysis showed that the demonstration had considerable net social payoff for the welfare mothers enrolled, primarily due to the long term earnings gains assumed and the value of the output from the demonstration jobs. Benefits also exceeded costs for the ex-addicts, in large part because of the reduction in socially destructive behavior (i.e., crime) and the gains in employment and earnings. For ex-convicts the results were less conclusive. The net benefit of the program may have been positive or negative depending on the assumptions used to value the benefits of the program. Not surprisingly in view of the estimated impact of the demonstration on youths, the program's cost was found to outweigh its benefits for the youth dropout group.

Because of the very specific nature of the treatment tested in the Supported Work Demonstration, it is difficult to draw broad policy conclusions from its results. The finding that the Supported Work approach had its greatest payoff in the case of AFDC mothers is consistent with a few other findings from the last decade of research on training and employment programs. Some of the studies of the Continuous Longitudinal Manpower Survey (CLMS) have also concluded that disadvantaged women helped by CETA appear to obtain the greatest program benefit. Similarly, in the Seattle-Denver experiment, the only group to show a positive impact from the counseling program (as distinct from the voucher program) was the sample of unmarried women with children. Also, as we shall see below, the Employment Opportunity Pilot Project appeared to have a more consistently and significantly positive effect on unmarried women than on other groups served. It would thus appear that single mothers are more susceptible to being helped by public training and employment efforts than other groups of hard-to-employ workers.

The Employment Opportunity Pilot Project

The history of the Employment Opportunity Pilot Project—or EOPP—was a tumultuous one, marked by shifting objectives and premature cancellation. It is said that we learn from our mistakes. If this were true, EOPP should have been one of the most richly informative demonstrations ever undertaken. The project was begun by the Carter Administration in order to estimate participation rates and potential effects of a guaranteed jobs program similar to that proposed in Carter's welfare reform package. Alarmed by the work effort reductions estimated in the Seattle-Denver experiment, the Administration was determined to limit the work disincentive effects of its welfare proposal by requiring certain welfare recipients to accept public service employment (PSE) if they were unable to obtain unsubsidized jobs. The President's welfare reform efforts were twice rebuffed by Congress, but his PSE proposals were treated more sympathetically. In 1978 Congress permitted the Department of Labor to set up a 14-site pilot test of a guaranteed jobs program.

Even before the first EOPP enrollments took place in 1979, the basic objectives of the demonstration had already been modified. This was due in part to the Administration's evolving objectives in reforming welfare and CETA. In addition to simply providing a test of the guaranteed jobs concept, which was expected to be very expensive, the architects of EOPP also hoped to test new approaches to job finding among the hard-core unemployed. If applicants for PSE jobs could be required to participate in intensive and structured programs of job finding, and if those programs turned out to be successful, the "demand" for PSE job slots, and hence the cost of PSE, could be limited.

At the time the demonstration began in 1979, its objective was to determine whether a program that provided a combination of ". . . job search assistance and subsidized employment and training could succeed in increasing the employment and, hence, reducing the welfare dependence of adults in low-income families with children. The program, targeted primarily toward families that were receiving AFDC, provided participants with intensive job search assistance and support services, such as child care and transportation assistance. Participants who were unsuccessful at finding an unsubsidized job after a prescribed period of active search were offered a subsidized job or training."[13]

When President Reagan took office in 1981, the goals of the program, or at least the focus of the program evaluation, shifted once again. The new Administration wished to abolish public service jobs, not to pilot test a program that guaranteed them. It emphatically signaled this goal by ending enrollments into EOPP's PSE jobs program, sharply curtailing enrollment in other components of the EOPP program, and prematurely terminating the entire project in October 1981, less than two-and-one-half years after operations began in 1979. Mathematica, the prime research contractor for the project, was directed to discover the impact, if any, of EOPP's job search assistance program and to provide a cost-benefit analysis of that program.

The implementation of EOPP and its evaluation were seriously harmed by these shifts in program objective. The original research and implementation design of EOPP was sensible for a pilot test of a guaranteed jobs program. However, it was extremely deficient for evaluating alternative approaches to job search assistance, the goal emphasized in the final evaluation contract. The available control group was ill-suited to examining job search assistance. To evaluate a guaranteed jobs program it is necessary to conduct saturation demonstrations under a variety of local labor market conditions. By saturation demonstrations we mean that the program had to be offered on an unlimited basis to all income-eligible families in a particular community. Saturation was required in order to determine participation rates in a well-publicized program and, equally important, to see whether such a program would seriously disrupt local labor markets by driving down the available supply of labor for unsubsidized employment. To see how local labor market conditions were affected by EOPP, it was necessary to obtain a basis for comparison. Mathematica and DOL officials selected 14 comparison sites to be used as a "control group" for the 14 pilot sites in the demonstration. (Because "control sites" were selected, EOPP might arguably be called an experiment rather than a demonstration project. However, eligibility for treatment was not randomly assigned to individuals except in Dayton and Philadelphia, and hence the project was probably closer to an ordinary demonstration than to a formal social experiment.) This strategy required massive amounts of household interviewing in both pilot and comparison sites.

Only a small proportion of these household interviews would have been needed for an adequate assessment of the job search assistance program by itself. Moreover, the experimental and control groups should have been randomly selected from the eligible population in the pilot sites. Indeed, for testing job search assistance, an experimental design involving at most a few thousand participants and controls in selected labor market environments is all that would have been required. Neither saturation, nor multiple control sites, nor massive interviewing would have been necessary.

EOPP was adminstered by the state and local officials (prime sponsors) responsible for administering local CETA programs. The competence and commitment of local administrators thus varied considerably. The prime sponsors were responsible for publicizing the availability of EOPP services, identifying, recruiting, and determining the technical eligibility of potential clients, providing support services like child care for enrolled participants, establishing and administering a structured program of job search assistance, and providing public service jobs, work experience slots, and classroom and on-the-job training opportunities for clients unable to obtain unsubsidized employment. The broad character of program responsibilities and the potential for administrative discretion at each point are noteworthy, and they threaten the reliability of evaluation findings. We simply cannot be confident about the exact nature of the treatment as delivered in the field.

EOPP tested self-directed job search methods that are quite distinct from the job referral and job development techniques usually used in the Employment Service or CETA. Clients were taught effective methods of job search and encouraged to follow a rigorous and structured routine in looking for employment. People who could not find unsubsidized jobs in five to eight weeks were offered a subsidized employment or training position, which could last up to one year before workers or trainees were recycled through the job search assistance program. Workers in PSE jobs and OJT training positions were paid regular wages, while those in work experience or classroom training slots were given a weekly training stipend.

To be eligible for EOPP job search assistance, applicants had to be adult members of families that included one or more children and that either received AFDC or had income below 70 percent of BLS's Lower Living Standard. To be eligibile for subsidized employment or training, individuals were required to complete the job search phase of the program without obtaining unsubsidized employment and, in addition, be the family's primary earner and either receive AFDC or have low enough income to qualify for AFDC. In most sites the program was aimed primarily at adult AFDC recipients.

Mathematica's evaluation of EOPP covers only 10 of the 14 communities involved in the demonstration. In those ten communities it is estimated that over 190,000 adults were eligible for EOPP services at some point during the demonstration.[14] However, of that total only 120,000 were eligible for the full range of EOPP services, including subsidized employment and training. Only 21,000—or 18 percent—of those fully eligible chose to enroll in EOPP. An additional 2,000 adults eligible only for job search assistance also enrolled in the program.[15] Of those individuals who filled out the forms to enroll, only about 62 percent remained in the program long enough to receive some job search assistance. One-third of the people receiving job search help obtained an unsubsidized job. Only 4,100—or 17 percent of enrollees—remained with the program long enough to receive subsidized employment or training, of which approximately two-thirds were assigned to PSE jobs.[16] Thus, of the 120,000 potential participants in EOPP's "guaranteed jobs" program, fewer than 3 percent actually obtained PSE jobs.

The striking feature of these statistics is the very small proportion of program eligibles who actually received program services, especially very expensive services like subsidized jobs and training. This suggests that a guaranteed public jobs program aimed at the welfare-eligible poor would be considerably less expensive than anticipated by the Carter Administration, which expected a much higher participation rate. On the other hand, the program would also be much less successful than expected in reducing welfare dependence, since only a small percentage of AFDC recipients would apparently be forced to participate in such a program.[17] In part the low participation rate in the jobs program was attributable to uncertain guidelines from the Labor Department, poor program administration at the local level, normal start-up problems, and a lack of publicity for the program. Even with these problems it was astonishing to program operators that so small a proportion of obviously eligible people chose to enroll. Among AFDC recipients who were mandatory participants in the WIN program (and thus likely to be ready to hold a job), only one-third enrolled in EOPP, and the availability of EOPP was widely advertised among that group.[18] Among nonrecipients of AFDC who were eligible for EOPP PSE jobs, only 8 percent enrolled in the EOPP program.[19]

In view of the apparently generous offer provided by the program, this studied indifference to EOPP is interesting. Of course, it is possible to keep enthusiasm for public jobs down by erecting enough bureaucratic hurdles—a complex and lengthy application process, mandatory participation in a job search program, and potentially lengthy delays before assignment to a PSE job. Nonetheless, it appears that the attractiveness of a temporary PSE job paying between one and two times the minimum wage is not nearly as great as sometimes assumed. Even though EOPP provided a highly imperfect test, the administration of the demonstration was probably not perceptibly inferior to what would be provided in an on-going program. The local administrators of the program were after all the same people responsible for administering CETA and are probably now running training and referral programs under JTPA. If there is any future consideration of a guaranteed jobs program for welfare recipients, EOPP has taught us that both the costs and benefits will be considerably below what was expected in the mid-1970s.

What of the other objectives of the project? The evaluation contractor concluded that the job search assistance program run by EOPP was probably effective in helping participants find jobs. Enrollees in the job search assistance program increased the amount and effectiveness of their search efforts. In comparison to unemployed workers in the target population who did not enroll in EOPP, participants spent nearly twice as many hours a week searching for a job, contacted about four times as many potential employers, and filed approximately 75 percent more formal job applications.[20] As mentioned earlier, about one-third of enrollees receiving job search help landed an unsubsidized job. Although it is unclear how much of an improvement is indicated by this placement rate, Mathematica concluded that for the largest group of enrollees—single mothers—EOPP probably raised the employment rate by 10 to 12 percentage points and raised the probability of *unsubsidized* employment by 7 to 9 percentage points.[21]

Because EOPP was so poorly designed to measure the effectiveness of job search assistance, Mathematica could not determine the fraction of the employment gain that was due solely to the job search plans tested. Nor were the researchers able to reliably measure the impact of EOPP on the other groups served—married women and men with dependent children. Mathematica could detect no impact of the program on welfare dependency, a surprising finding in view of the population served by EOPP, which consisted overwhelmingly of public assistance recipients. Because EOPP and its evaluation were terminated with unseemly haste in 1981, we will never know whether the employment gains registered by EOPP participants were temporary or long-lasting. Nor can we ascertain whether welfare dependency was eventually affected by the program. Because of the limitations described above, Mathematica was unable to perform a benefit-cost analysis of the job search program alone, although the analysts did conclude that the EOPP project's overall social benefits probably exceeded its social costs. Based on our reading of the evidence, it appears that a modest and comparatively inexpensive program to help low-income breadwinners search for work may reduce spells of unemployment and raise the fraction of time spent working. Even though it is doubtful that this kind of help will change many workers' lives or radically change the nature of jobs they obtain, the help is nonetheless worthwhile, and it comes at relatively low cost.

Before concluding this discussion of EOPP, we should also note that some of the pilot sites tested variants of the basic self-directed job search model. One of the most interesting variants was tested in Dayton, Ohio where wage-subsidy vouchers were distributed to a randomly selected subgroup of enrollees in the job search classes. The vouchers were simply certificates provided to participants to help them in their search for work. Participants were encouraged to alert potential employers of their vouchered status. If a vouchered job seeker was hired by a qualified employer, the employer could claim a subsidy for a fraction of the wages paid to the newly hired worker. The subsidy was payable either in the form of a tax credit or a direct check payment to the employer. It was worth up to $4,500 over a 2-year period.

In effect, the vouchered workers were "on sale." Employers, however, appeared to regard these workers as damaged goods. In comparison to unvouchered participants in the EOPP program, vouchered job seekers were significantly less likely to obtain employment during their 5- or 8-week job search period. Although this experiment is limited in many ways, and the research on it was discontinued too early to be definitive, the findings are intriguing. The basic result appears to show that a targeted wage voucher may hurt rather than help a job seeker's chances of employment. It should thus come as no surprise that our nation's two most important wage subsidy programs—the WIN and Targeted Jobs tax credits—are so little used. Because the stigma associated with these programs may outweigh their tax advantages to employers, the unemployed may be reluctant to use them and employers may be less likely to hire job seekers who offer them.

A Moral and Some Lessons

Social experiments have primarily been tools of social scientists seeking guidance for effective policy reform or innovation, but their conclusions have often been very pessimistic for those wishing to change public policy. According to the Foreword of the *New Jersey Income Maintenance Experiment* final report, the decision to undertake that experiment was based on the ". . . rapid spread of the belief, especially among economists, that negative income taxation was an idea whose time had come."[22] After the New Jersey Experiment began, two Presidents—Nixon and Carter—proposed variants of a federal negative income tax, but in neither case was the cause of the proposal advanced by findings from the experiments. In fact, the high price tag of the proposed Carter plan, which certainly harmed its chances of enactment, was estimated using interim results from the Seattle-Denver experiment.

Because of the rigor with which experiments are designed and evaluated there may be a bias toward reaching pessimistic conclusions about policies that are experimentally tested. The tested program is subject to critical examination of a type that is rarely imposed on existing programs. Such an examination is likely to reveal undesirable or even pernicious side-effects of a policy that might not otherwise be detected. Consider, for example, the earned income tax credit. Under this apparently benign provision of the tax code, refundable tax credits are provided to low-wage workers who have dependents. The purpose of the credit is to encourage work effort. If this policy were systematically evaluated using the methods applied to social experiments, the credit might be shown to reduce work effort or encourage family dissolution as the NIT was found to do. Indeed, the credit increases work disincentives because it increases marginal tax rates for more workers than are eligible for a subsidy on marginal work. If these effects were found to occur, and if they were widely publicized, the credit could be politically doomed. However, such effects are unlikely to be investigated because of the program's uncontroversial nature.

Numerous other examples could be mentioned. Do subsidized student loans stimulate increases in education? If they do, is the added investment in education worth its social and private cost? Do business tax reductions and other state-local subsidy programs to attract new business achieve their goals? Such programs could conceivably reduce or delay local investment projects if businesses delayed their decisions as a result of their efforts to attract subsidy support.

If an experimentally tested program fails to achieve its intended purpose, or if it has disagreeable consequences, those facts can be demonstrated with statistical rigor. Even more disturbing, if the program fails to achieve spectacular positive results, the degree to which it falls short of perfection can be measured precisely and then used as an argument against its implementation. If on the other hand an on-going program does not achieve its objectives or does harm, its failure may remain unsuspected, or at least unproved.

As an empirical fact, politically divisive policies are the ones most likely to be subject to rigorous experimentation—negative income taxation, housing vouchers for the poor, national health insurance, and labor market assistance to low-income workers. Programs aiding the able-bodied poor are among those with the weakest popular mandate, and hence their reform will nearly always inspire deep controversy. It is unclear whether experimentation *per se* can shed much light on the main points at issue—the demands of equity, the nature of a fair distribution, and the limit of society's obligation to help those who are at least partly able to help themselves. Our experience in the last fifteen years has taught us that large-scale social experiments can be relied on to teach us something of value about the policy in question, but what we are taught can seldom be relied on to aid the cause of reforming or improving policy. Since society is not even-handed in subjecting programs for the poor and nonpoor to experimental investigation, we should not be surprised that experimental scrutiny has been less than kind to programs for the poor. There is a moral here, and it is illustrated in the three experiments we have considered: if you advocate a particular policy reform or innovation, do not press to have it tested.

Beyond this political economy moral, are there lessons for research or evaluation that can be gleaned from the experiments? One such lesson concerns the costs and benefits of large-scale social experimentation relative to nonexperimental social research. Clearly, the research costs of social experimentation are enormous. For the three experiments reviewed here, the costs of program administration (including experimental transfers, stipends, and wages) and evaluation exceeded $200 million. The potential benefits in terms of additions to knowledge may also be substantial, especially when it is recognized that obtaining reliable information about human behavior is usually a slow process. However, if the opportunity cost of any proposed experiment is a reduction in nonexperimental research costing the same amount of money, the expected findings would have to be extremely valuable for the benefits of an experiment to exceed its cost. Of course, this conclusion is weaker if the opportunity cost of the resources used for experimentation is low. This would be the case, for example, for resources that are diverted from some activity with low social value.

In view of the high cost of experiments, it is appropriate to subject proposals for future experiments to a test that includes the following questions:

1. Have adequate models of the behavior which the experimental treatment is designed to affect been developed and tested on existing bodies of data?

2. Can the experiment and its evaluation meet high standards of basic research? That is, can problems of time horizon, contamination, Hawthorne effects, replicability, and extrapolation of results to a national program be handled adequately in the experimental design or in the evaluation of experimental results?

3. Can the experiment provide evidence about a social policy that cannot be obtained using less expensive, nonexperimental methods? Alternatively, can the experiment provide findings that are sufficiently more reliable or statistically precise to justify the added cost of the research?

4. How important are the potential research findings about experimental outcomes? Are they crucial in determining whether the tested treatment is a good or bad policy?

5. Can the experiment permit tests and evaluation of the operational feasibility of social policy measures and yield evidence on the effectiveness of alternative administrative arrangements of such programs?

6. Can the experimental findings be validly generalized to infer the consequences of policies not specifically tested in the experiment?

The number of potential social experiments that can pass the test implied by these questions is not likely to be large. This conclusion is strengthened by our review of the findings of the three experiments. While the evidence on behavioral responses is more reliable than is likely to be obtained from nonexperimental research, its value, in terms of added knowledge per dollar of cost, was not uniquely high except in the case of the tested NIT plans. For the training and employment experiments, including the one run as part of the Seattle-Denver experiment, the programs tested were so specific in nature that it is difficult to extrapolate the findings except to other programs that are run exactly as they were. (For EOPP, even this may be impossible because the tested treatments are essentially nonreplicable.)

The NIT experiment was more valuable for two reasons. Its findings were considerably more reliable and statistically precise than any that had been obtained in the preceding 10 years of nonexperimental research. Moreover, its findings are useful in evaluating tax and welfare policies in addition to those actually tested in Seattle-Denver, in part because there is a well-developed theory for assessing labor supply responses to tax rates and guarantees.

But the exception represented by the Seattle-Denver experiment is rare. Many conceivable experiments in the field of employment and training must concentrate on testing "black box" treatments. Supported Work and the job club model tested in EOPP both represent this kind of treatment. There is no well-established theory, as existed in the case of the NIT experiments, that permits us to predict whether and how these particular approaches will affect participants. Nor can we predict from experimental findings the effect of similar—but not identical—policy options. This lack of knowledge regarding the process by which treatment affects performance limits the applicability of the findings. In the case of both Supported Work and EOPP, the treatment tested was of little interest by the time the research was completed, and the findings, in turn, were of limited value in assessing policy options then being considered.

Black box experiments can be valuable in employment and training research if they are relatively inexpensive but rigorous and if there is systematic variation in the treatments which are tested. Investing large sums of money to test a single approach is likely to be a serious error except under very unusual conditions. To justify its high cost, a social experiment must offer the prospect of valuable additions to knowledge about human behavior. In light of the moral mentioned above, the benefits of an experiment will seldom include basic reforms to policy.

NOTES

1. A very small number of families were enrolled in experimental plans lasting up to 20 years.

2. Office of Income Security Policy, U.S. Department of Health and Human Services, *Overview of the Seattle-Denver Income Maintenance Experiment Final Report,* Government Printing Office, Washington, DC, 1983, pp. 13-16. The higher estimate of the impact on women heading single-parent families is based on the responses of women in the 5-year group during the fourth and fifth experimental years. Remaining estimates are based on reported responses of enrollees in both the 3- and 5-year groups during the second and third experimental years.

3. Ibid., p. 6.

4. See Henry Aaron and John Todd, "The Use of Income Maintenance Experiment Findings in Public Policy, 1977-78." *Industrial Relations Research Association Proceedings,* 1979, pp. 46-56.

5. Implementing a NIT program for single-parent families, given the combination of existing transfer programs, is difficult. Because of the widely varying AFDC benefit levels across states, it is difficult to select a NIT guarantee level that is low enough to be affordable, but high enough so that only a small fraction of families in the high-benefit states receive a NIT payment that is no lower than their current benefit. A national NIT plan with a guarantee equal to three-quarters of the poverty line would increase labor supply among single mothers, not because of the work incentive embodied in a low tax rate, but because transfer benefits would be slashed for so many mothers in states currently paying high benefits.

6. This result as well as those reported in the preceding paragraph are from Philip K. Robins and Richard W. West, "Labor Supply Response," in *Final Report of the Seattle-Denver Income Maintenance Experiment,* vol. I, *Design and Results,* U.S. Department of Health and Human Services, Government Printing Office, pp. 180-87.

7. Strictly speaking, the experiment provided no evidence about the impact of raising marginal tax rates to 100 percent. Within the range of tax rates tested in the experiment, however, higher tax rates appear to be associated with higher aggregate labor supply. See Ibid., p. 182.

8. Assignments to the employment-training programs were conducted in such a way that analysts were able to reliably distinguish the separate impacts of those programs and the tested NIT plans.

9. Reimbursable (or direct) expenses included costs for tuition, books, transportation, and child care.

10. Note that this was the impact on program *eligibles;* the impact on program *participants* was of course much greater. The 50 percent subsidy also encouraged some extra schooling, but the increases were smaller. See Bureau of Social Science Research, *Vouchering Manpower Services: Past Experiences and Their Implications for Future Programs,* Bureau of Social Science Research report to the National Commission on Employment Policy, Washington, DC, 1982, p. 20.

11. Ibid., p. 29.

12. This quote as well as much of the material for this section is drawn from Manpower Demonstration Research Corporation, *Summary and the Findings of the National Supported Work Demonstration,* Ballinger Publishing Co., Cambridge, MA, 1980.

13. Mathematica Policy Research, *Final Report: Employment Opportunity Pilot Project: Analysis of Program Impacts,* MPR, Princeton, NJ, p. 1.

14. Ibid., p. 20.

15. Ibid., p. 22.

16. Ibid., pp. 27, 105 and 116.

17. We should emphasize that the low participation of welfare recipients in the demonstration was partly attributable to poor enforcement of job search requirements in local welfare departments. If the job search/PSE jobs and welfare programs were more tightly coordinated, the costs and hence potential benefits of an EOPP-type program might have been greater.

18. Mathematica Policy Research, *Final Report,* p. 22. Many mandatory participants in WIN are in fact required to participate in an activity like EOPP as a condition for continued receipt of welfare benefits.

19. Ibid., p. 22.

20. Ibid., p. 108.

21. Ibid., p. 3. A small percentage of enrollees obtained employment in EOPP's own jobs program. For that reason the gains in unsubsidized employment were smaller than those in all forms of employment.

22. David Kershaw and Jerilyn Fair, *The New Jersey Income Maintenance Experiment,* Volume I, *Operations, Surveys, and Administration,* Academic Press, New York, 1976, p. xi.